VW BEETLE

Custom Handbook

This book is dedicated to Tim Sneller who,
in his all too short life,
shared my passion for the Bug.

VW BEETLE

Custom Handbook

Keith Seume

BAY VIEW BOOKS

First published 1989 by
Bay View Books Ltd
13a Bridgeland Street
Bideford, Devon EX39 2QE

Editor Charles Herridge
Designer Gerrard Lindley

ISBN 1 870979 10 9
Printed in Hong Kong

The author wishes to express his gratitude to the following people (listed in alphabetical order of course!), all of whom contributed more than he can ever thank them for:

Alan Arnold (UVA Ltd); John Brewster (Autocavan); Terry Grimwood; Barry Haselock (House of Haselock); Link House Magazines Ltd; Jacky Morel (Super VW Magazine); Brian Noto (VW Trends) and Geoff Thomas (Autocavan – thanks for all those hours in the workshop!)

Two especially big 'thanks' go to Mike and June Key for all their kindness and generosity in digging me out of a hole with photos!

The biggest 'thanks' goes to Gwynn – the one person who had to put up with my 'eleventh hour' style of writing! Thanks one and all.

CONTENTS

WHY ALL THE FUSS?

Just what is it about the Beetle?

When all things are considered, the odds were pretty heavily stacked against the Beetle ever seeing the light of day, let alone becoming a cult car of any description.

When the order was given to design a car for the people, one that would allow Herr Schmidt and his family to cruise into a new world along Germany's autobahn network, many ideas were tossed on the table. Only one saw the light of day: the KdF-Wagen, the 'Strength Through Joy' car.

The successful designer was Dr Ferdinand Porsche and his concept was for a rounded, almost aerodynamic, vehicle mounted on a flat floorpan with torsion bar suspension at front and rear. Power came from an ingenious horizontally-opposed four-cylinder engine cooled by air blown over the cylinders by a cooling fan mounted on the generator shaft.

The reasoning behind the suspension layout was that, by mounting the torsion bars transversely across the car, the designer could gain more interior space for the passengers. Torsion bars are also by nature rising rate springs – i.e. the more you try to deform them, the stiffer

they become. This is exactly what a lightweight vehicle needs, for if heavy springs are fitted then the ride becomes objectionably firm, while if they are too light then handling will be poor when the vehicle is heavily loaded.

As for the engine, Porsche had been experimenting with similar ideas for many years, even designing a four-cylinder air-cooled engine for Austro-Daimler as far back as 1912. The shape of the car was born out of Porsche's fascination with the streamlined race cars of Benz, and with the Rumpler Tropfenwagen, a teardrop-shaped machine that for the first time exploited nature's most perfect form, the raindrop.

right
The Beetle is the one car in the world that everyone can identify, its shape is as unique as the Coke bottle.

below
Fast Four Veedubs – one of literally thousands of Volkswagen clubs all over the world. No other car has such a huge worldwide following.

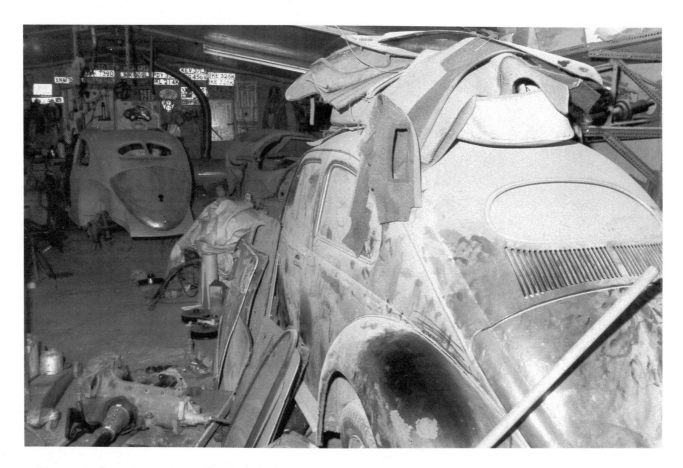

However, Porsche soon realized that there was another great benefit to be derived from the curving of body panels – the car becomes much stronger. As Volkswagen themselves suggested in their advertising almost thirty years later, try tapping a few rival body panels. Few can withstand pressure like the Bug's suit of armour.

To enable the German public to purchase the new People's Car (the literal translation of Volkswagen), Hitler introduced a savings scheme whereby each family could buy stamps to fill a book. When the book was full, you got another until eventually you had supposedly raised enough money to take possession of your Beetle. Or so the idea went. The truth was rather different: before World War II not one single Volkswagen was delivered to a private individual, the few vehicles that were produced being grabbed by the military and by party leaders.

However, although never conceived as a military vehicle at the outset, the Beetle soon won admiration for its ruggedness and dependability. Military versions were designed, including a four-wheel-drive version that pre-dated modern thinking by thirty years. The most significant wartime development was the Kubelwagen (Bucket Car!) which became the mainstay of the German army throughout the conflict – very much the Jeep of Germany.

Had the Allied forces not come to the conclusion that the Volkswagen factory at Wolfsburg (a town built solely for the factory workers) was responsible for producing some of Hitler's infamous V1 'Flying Bombs', it might have escaped obliteration bombing, but then there might not have been the same twist to the tale.

Major Ivan Hirst of the Royal Electrical and Mechanical Engineers was brought in to assess the

above
Just what is it that makes a perfectly sane person want to tear apart, restore and then cherish a thirty-year-old VW? There has to be something.

top right
It didn't take long for somebody somewhere to get out a saw and cut the front off his Bug to make the first Baja Bug like this early British one.

bottom right
Well, they say customizing is an expression of the owner's taste, and all that can be said about this example is that it's certainly different.

possibility of restarting production at the factory after hostilities ceased in 1945. Already it had been noted that the Volkswagen offered useful possibilities in war-torn Germany as transport for the Allied forces. Hirst rooted around and soon began to pull the Volkswagen out of the ashes and back into the daylight it had thought it would never see again. The first cars thus produced were built out of whatever happened to be left undamaged in the ruins of the factory, but it soon became obvious that supplies of vital parts would run out before long.

One cloud which sat firmly on the horizon was the Allies' intention to dismantle all war-related manufacturing facilities and thus prevent rearmament by the German forces. Because the Volkswagen had been very much part of the war effort, it looked for a while as if the Beetle would find itself without a factory. However, the factory was placed in the hands of the Property Control section of the Control Commission for Germany, which fortunately realized the need for transportation. A four-year period of grace was granted to the factory and, as time would prove, the plan was

People do the craziest things with their Beetles. This Swedish
owner cut and shut his Bug until it was waist-high. One radical
Volkswagen . . .

abandoned before the axe fell on Wolfsburg and the Bug.

Henry Ford and Sir William Rootes were shown the factory and virtually offered it on a plate, but both turned it down as not being a viable proposition, so it was left to stand on its own two feet. History has proved that these two gentlemen had remarkably poor foresight . . .

The Beetle may have had this extraordinary history but there is still no obvious reason why it should have gone on to be so successful, especially in markets, like America, where the taste was for larger luxury cars.

When the first Beetles were exported to foreign countries, the response varied from amazement to sheer disbelief. Never before had there been a car that looked like the Bug (a name soon hung on the poor car by the American populace), drove like the Bug or indeed sounded like the Bug. In a world that lived by the term 'bigger and better', the Volkswagen seemed hopelessly out of place. It was only when tales started to emerge about its tremendous dependability, lack of thirst and high cruising speed (the Bug had always been designed to cruise at its maximum speed) that interest rose. It was the perfect car for the average low-income family, or for the wife at home to take the kids to school in. It all started to make sense.

Among the engineering fraternity, the torsion bar suspension earned a lot of respect, as did the watch-like engine. To quote from a 1958 manual on how to modify your VW for speed (!), 'The VW's appeal lies in the fact that it is an honest car; it does not pretend to be what it isn't. Every part of the VW has been designed to perform a duty, just like every part of an airplane had been designed to be functional. In fact many fundamentals of aircraft practice are also found on the VW; to mention but a few: functionality, lightness, efficiency, air cooling and quality.

'In short, even if to some the VW could not lay claim to be the most beautiful car in the world, it is an honest, functional, reliable and endearing piece of machinery. And last, but by no means least, it is excellent value for the money.' Thank you Henry Elfrink – I couldn't have put it better myself.

left
Who would have thought that the Bug would go racing? From the earliest days the VW was respected for its strength. This Baja racer looks tough.

above
Even the much desired Cabriolet comes in for some attention. The flared fenders and whitewall tires date this Bug – it is from the late 1970s.

Few cars can boast having so many Tee-shirts designed around them. There is a stream of new designs every year — and they all sell!

Over the years there have been thousands of toys based upon the Beetle. This is part of a collection in France totaling over two thousand models.

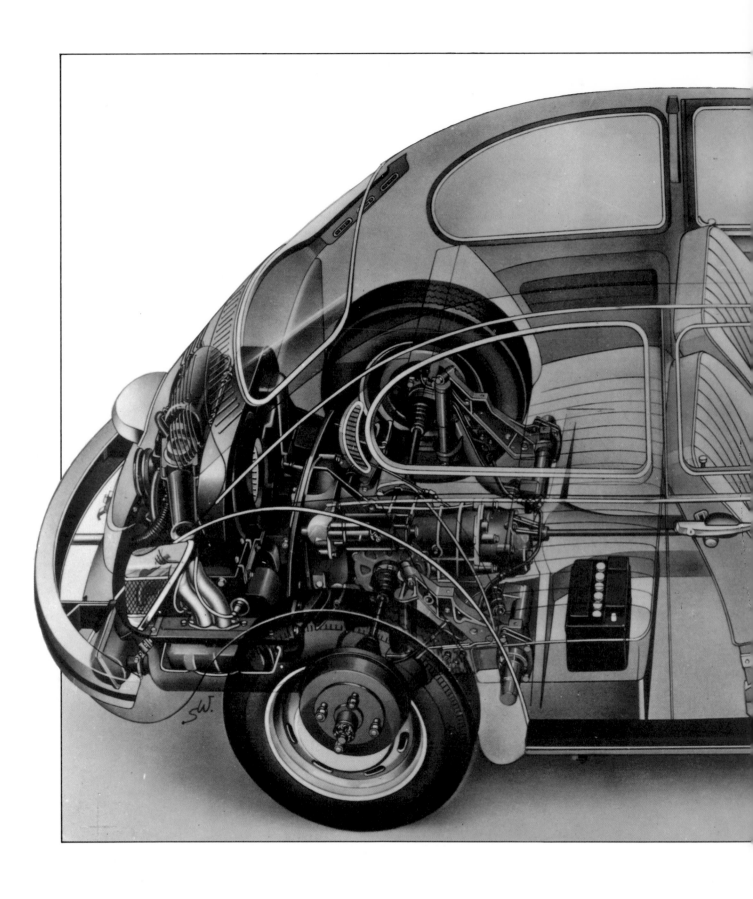

The beauty of a Bug is not just skin deep: this cutaway drawing of a late Super Beetle shows just how rugged the Volkswagen Beetle really is.

High'n'mighty, this much modified Beetle is something of a mobile mutant! It looks more like a radio-controlled toy than a real vehicle.

But all this still doesn't answer the question why so many people have modified Beetles, raced Beetles, built Buggies, chopped the fenders off to make Bajas, chopped the roof off to make Roadsters – even made them watertight to make them float (and swim)! Why does the Beetle have so strong an appeal that Walt Disney made a film hero out of one? Could Herbie have been anything other than a Beetle? Would the film have had the same appeal if it had been called 'Herbie the Edsel'? I doubt it.

For one thing, the shape is universally recognizable – just like the Coke bottle or Concorde. It has the look of a cute little cuddly toy from the front, an engine that sounds like a sewing machine and a character that overwhelms you as soon as you settle down behind the wheel. Everything about the Beetle is unique – and its connections with Porsche don't hurt any either!

It is impossible to say who was the first person ever to take the body off a Beetle and drive the floorpan on a beach. It must have happened a long time ago, and I bet he didn't know what he was in at the beginning of. We know who was the first to come up with a 'glass body for a

Buggy – that was Bruce Meyers – but who first cut the fenders off a Bug to make a Baja? Many people have claimed that honour, but it would be impossible to prove.

When it comes to California Look, it is generally reckoned that Greg Aronson and friends were the first to drop the front, strip the chrome and slip in a hot Webered motor. On the drag strips it was Joe and Darrell Vittone who took the early glories in their 'Inch Pincher' sedan.

But all this still doesn't answer the question, why the Beetle? On a personal level, I can remember the first Bug I ever saw regularly. I walked past it on the way to school each day and it was a split-window model in red. The guy sold it a few months later and bought a black one. I was fascinated by the shape of this thing when at the time everyone else was driving very upright, old-

top right
A lot of owners spend a fortune on having their pride and joy restored professionally. Extensive anti-corrosion measures ensure a long life.

bottom right
What other car tempts the owner to carry out a conversion to make it look like a forty-year-old example? Split-window kit is popular.

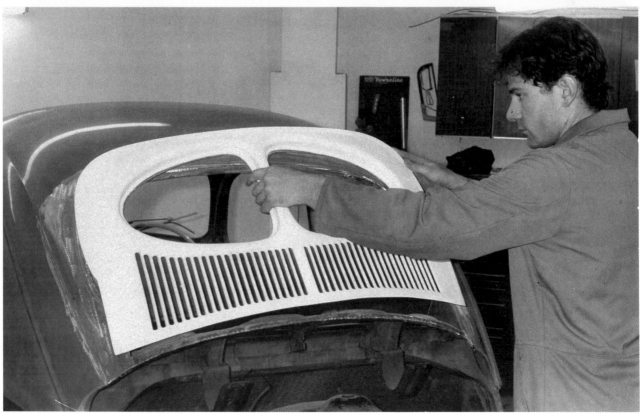

left
Drag racing a VW? The seemingly humble Bug has proved itself a winner on strips across the world. Rear-mounted engine is the secret of success.

below
No matter how rugged the VW might be, there are some situations where even a Bug-based machine can get stuck! This off-road rail has problems.

fashioned (or so it seemed to me) automobiles. Somehow it looked right, in an undefinable sort of way.

When my older brother went off to university a few years later, he came back after the first term raving about the fun he had been having with a friend in his '62 Ruby Red Beetle. The guy was a farmer's son and was used to driving the Bug all over the farm. He soon learnt that it didn't get stuck very easily. He took delight in showing off his car's attributes to my amazed brother, who at the time was driving an Austin Minivan.

When this friend, Glenn Scott, came to visit in his Bug, he took me out in it and tackled some slopes I didn't believe could be climbed in anything other than a four-by-four. I was hooked, but too young to drive. My biggest thrill was when Glenn stopped by one day and said, 'Do you want to drive?' I must have been all of twelve or thirteen. I guess we reached a best of about 15mph, but I couldn't stop thinking about it – and still recall that the first car I ever drove was a Bug.

My brother bought himself a '59 (a Garnet Red one with a damaged left front fender), and then went on to own a pair of Pearl White '64s. The first of these was hit by a Jaguar one day at an intersection. The Jaguar's engine mountings broke. I was impressed.

Beetle ownership came my way, after a couple of false starts with a Fiat and a Renault (both rear-engined!), in the form of a Swiss '63 sedan with a factory sunroof. That got modified and lowered (in 1975) and in turn made way for a '67 1500 which also got the treatment. A '54 body was dropped onto a '67 floorpan for some fun with a hot 1700cc engine, and even now, many years later, the call of the Bug is still too strong to ignore.

But the great unanswered question remains: why the Bug? For me the appeal is that they are unique in every respect. They are idiosyncratic, they have a mind of their own (especially when it comes to starting a six-volt Bug on a cold morning), they are the only cars I have ever driven that provoke other owners into waving at me (but why?) and I love the people that drive them. Beetle owners are sincere and helpful. Some say they are crazy, but being crazy is not so bad.

I hope you enjoy reading this book as much as I have enjoyed putting it together. It is not the definitive manual on race-tuning your Bug, or how to win the Baja 1000 in your Buggy. What I hope it does is stimulate some thoughts, prove that buying a Bug is a good idea, show that a rusty Bug isn't the end of the world and suggest how you can make the Bug into something special – I dare not say unique, because it already is. Have fun!

The license plate that says it all! Owning a low-riding Cal Look
Bug is what every young Veedub fanatic dreams of.

Anyone who thinks Beetles are boring has never attended a
VW show and taken in the radical graphics that are so much
part of the scene today.

BIRTH OF THE BEETLE
From split windows to MacPherson struts

Although the word 'Volkswagen' summons up a universal image of what we know and love as the Beetle or Bug, few people outside the VW world have any real idea of just how different the last of the line Super Beetles are from the very early production models. Sure, they all have that cute humpy shape that has been immortalized in everything from toys to toilet roll holders, but under the skin – and indeed all over it – there have been hundreds of changes through the years. While it is not the intention of this book to bring you the definitive history of the VW Beetle and detail every change made since its inception, it is important that the prospective purchaser of a VW should be aware of the significant changes made during the Beetle's life.

Unless you are one of those absurdly fortunate people who go through life opening barn doors and stumbling across forgotten treasures, the chances are that you will be unlikely to find an undocumented Bug earlier than 1949 for sale. Sure, older ones do crop up now and again, but don't hold your breath waiting! Prior to this date, the cars produced were primarily destined for the home market, so few are to be found outside Germany.

It is important to note that Volkswagen, in common with many other manufacturers, often introduced new models in August. This can cause confusion because frequently enthusiasts will refer to, for example, a car built after August 1960 as a 1961 model. While it is true that the new models were introduced ready for the following year, the fact that they appeared in August of the 'old' year makes them technically that year's products. We have used December 31st/January 1st as the cut-off date each year in most of this chapter for the sake of simplicity. It is only when we get on to the 'new' Mexican-built Bugs of the '80s that we are forced to revert to a model year cut-off in the text. So please bear this in mind when checking out your new Bug. Where significant changes have occurred, rest assured that the chassis number has been quoted in each case to prevent even greater confusion! So, back to those desirable '49ers . . .

All models at this time had the split rear window, an 1131cc engine and a total lack of chromework. Brake operation was by cable and austerity was the order of the day. In 1949 (on the eighth day of the year to be precise) the very first Beetle began its trip to the USA via Holland. Chassis numbers started that year at 091922 and went on to 1-0138554, while engine numbers commenced with 1-0122650 and concluded with 1-0169913. The latter number is to be found stamped on the engine case below the generator. Models prior to

October 1949 were equipped with a starting handle, the dog for which can be seen on the crankshaft pulley bolt.

The instrument panel now sported a removable blanking plate to allow the installation of a radio or a clock without having to cut the metalwork as previously had been the case. The trunk could now be opened by a Bowden cable from inside the car; previously a locking handle was used. Export models used a high-gloss paint, this being a synthetic-based paint as opposed to the original cellulose type. These models also featured some chrome trim for the first time on a VW, along with reshaped overriders on the bumpers.

In 1950 (chassis numbers 1-0138555 to 1-0220133 and engine numbers 1-0169914 to 1-0265999), a rag-top (sunroof) model was offered for the first time. The wind-down window glass had small cut-outs in the leading edge to aid ventilation, no quarter-lights being fitted. Inside, the export models featured an ashtray on the dashboard and another on the rear side panel. Apart from numerous minor mechanical improvements, that's about all you get to identify a '50 from a '49. Check those chassis numbers!

In 1951 (chassis numbers 1-0220134 to 1-0313829 and engine numbers 266000 to 379470) the most significant and instantly recognizable change was the incorporation of a pair of ventilation flaps, one each side, in the front quarter panels ahead of the doors. Internally, the Beetle lost its standard bolster cushions for rear seat passengers in November of that year. Few other major changes happened that make the '51s different, but those vent flaps each side give the game away.

For 1952 (chassis numbers 1-0313830 to 1-0428156 and engine numbers 1-0379471 to 1-0519258) quarter-lights took the place of the previous single-pane glass in the doors. Rear lights now had top-mounted lenses for brake lights. The export model gained chrome trim down the trunk lid and extra trim round the windows. The engine compartment lid got a different handle – the familiar T-handle replacing the old single-blade type. At the front, too, a new trunk lid handle was fitted. By now 41.4% of all Beetles were being exported.

In 1953 (chassis numbers 1-0428157 to 1-0575414 and engine numbers 1-0519259 to 1-0695281) the first significant design change was made to the Bug – it lost the two little rear screens that made up the split-window of old and gained a new one-piece oval shaped screen. This momentous occasion took place with chassis number 1-0454951 and doubtless caused the downfall of many older cars as their owners wanted to convert the two 'splits' to a single 'oval'. The mind boggles at such destruction, but it did alas take place. Under the trunk lid, a larger diameter fuel filler cap could now be seen (it literally doubled in size from 40mm to 80mm).

In 1954 (chassis numbers 1-0575415 to 1-0781884 and engine numbers 1-0695282 to 1-0945526), VW went mad and increased the power output of the engine by 20%! This was achieved with a capacity increase from 1131cc to 1192cc and can be found on engine numbers commencing 1-0702742 (August 31st). To go along with this new engine, VW added a vacuum take-off to the carburetor to allow the use of a vacuum advance distributor. The exhaust system retained a solitary tailpipe exiting under the rear skirt, as on all previous models. Aside from various changes to the electrical and heating systems, that is the sum total of alterations made that year.

right
The '30-horse' engine of 1192cc featured a two-piece casting for the crankcase with integral mounting for the dynamo. Note tiny air filter.

below
Split-window on the right, oval-window on the left. Cabriolet model in the centre was produced from the earliest days of the Beetle's life.

The most famous rear window of all time? The split-window models were produced until the beginnning of 1953. That was the first 'oval' year.

opposite, top
Ulf Kaijser's much accessorized oval-window carries many period extras. There was a large market for parts like this during the '50s and '60s.

opposite, bottom
Interior of oval-window model featured simple dashboard with small glove box on opposite side to driver. Note cranked shifter and flower vase!

The year 1955 (chassis numbers from 1-0781885 to 1-1060929 and engine numbers from 1-0945527 to 1-1277347) saw one major change that helps to identify whether a Bug is a pre-'55 or '55-on: twin exhaust tailpipes now exited through cutouts in the rear skirt. Not only did this new exhaust system prove more efficient, it gave greater ground clearance and improved heating. Under the trunk lid, the fuel tank filler was redesigned with a smaller cap and a lower overall profile to improve luggage capacity. Detail interior changes included relocation of the heating controls, a cranked and relocated gear shift and redesigned front seats with adjustable backrests. Interior door trims were changed on export models – they now had leatherette strips at the top. The rear lights lost their separate brakelight lenses, and US-specification models were fitted with flashing turn signals from chassis number 1-0847967, requiring new rear quarter panel pressings to dispense with the slots for the semaphore-type indicators.

In 1956 (chassis numbers from 1-1060930 to 1-1394119 and engine numbers 1-1277348 to 1-1678209) there were no significant changes to the Bug. An external mirror became standard and some cars were fitted with tubeless tires for the first time. The VW logo on the

hubcaps came in black only – earlier models had colored logos to match the paintwork. The starter and windshield wiper motors were uprated.

The following year, 1957, (chassis numbers 1-1394120 to 1-1774680 and engine numbers from 1-1678210 to 1-2156321) produced no significant changes until August. So it was the 1958 model year (commencing in August '57) which saw the introduction of a greatly enlarged rear window, along with a windshield of enlarged proportions to match. From chassis number 1-1600440 onwards, the new rear window gave a massive 95% increase in glass area. The dashboard was completely redesigned, with an asymmetrical styling that was to continue virtually unchanged through to the last days of the Bug. Note too the 'organ pedal' throttle instead of the idiosyncratic roller pedal of old. The desirable 'W' deck lid was replaced with a less contoured type at the same time.

The year 1958 (from chassis number 1-774681 to 1-2226206 and engine numbers 1-2156322 to 1-2721313) saw few changes worthy of mention – every alteration made was of a detail nature, such as reducing the size of the heads of the bolts holding the fenders on to the main body from 14mm to 13mm (bet that sold a bunch more

cars!) and fitting a magnetic drainplug to the sump. The factory obviously thought the new rear window was enough to be getting along with.

In 1959 (chassis numbers from 1-2226207 to 1-2801613 and engine numbers from 1-2721314 to 1-2801613) again there were few significant changes. Identification points are the new door handles, with push buttons to open them, in place of the old pull type handles (from chassis number 1-2528668). A front anti-roll bar was introduced as standard on all models. Under the rear seat, kick panels were fitted to seal off the battery from the passenger compartment. In August a new steering wheel was introduced, with a semi-circular horn ring replacing the former horn button in the centre of the wheel. For those contemplating fitting a late engine into an early car, note that the angle of the engine and transmission was changed this year, allowing a little more space to fit things.

At this point, to prevent unnecessary confusion, we shall stop quoting engine numbers for each year, as the factory was about to introduce a new engine of increased power, while still offering the old engine, according to the market. We would be into quoting two sets of engine numbers at a time and, as we progress into the sixties, *three or four* at a time.

The year 1960 (chassis numbers 1-2801614 to 1-3551044) saw the introduction of a whole new engine, the 34bhp (40HP) 1192cc unit. This found its way into Bugs in August 1960 and commenced with the engine number 1-5000001. The easiest way to tell at a glance if your Bug has a pre-August '60 engine fitted is to note whether the generator mounting is a single casting in with the crankcase. Later engines have a separate casting affixed to the crankcase with four studs and nuts. The engine number is to be found on the crankcase below the generator mounting. At the same time, a new transmission was fitted featuring a one-piece casing. A damper was fitted to the steering assembly. At last the semaphore indicators disappeared, to be replaced by flashing turn signals on top of the front fenders and combined brakelight/turn signals at the rear. A windshield washer system was made standard on all models and the transmission now had synchromesh on all forward gears.

In 1961 (chassis numbers 1-3551045 to 1-4400051) we find the introduction on export models of a fuel gauge as standard (replacing the former reserve tap on the floor), along with a separate turn signal light on the rear light lens, introduced in August ready for '62. A worthwhile improvement was also made to the trunk lid: in place of the original single strut a pair of spring-loaded hinges were used to hold the lid open. Earlier models frequently suffered from split trunk lids adjacent to the strut fixing.

The next year, 1962, (chassis numbers 1-4400052 to 1-5225042) saw the introduction in December (from chassis number 1-5199981) of the so-called fresh-air heating system. Previously, air for the heater had been warmed by passing it over the cylinders, frequently resulting in an oily smell inside the car, but the new design meant that the heat exchangers were used, keeping air 'fresh' at all times (until they rusted through . . .). Few other significant changes occurred in that year.

In 1963 (chassis numbers 1-5225043 to 1-6016120) the front turn signals were increased in size from chassis number 1-5888185 and the rear licence plate light was widened, with a corresponding change in the contours of the engine lid. The latter change came in August. The hubcaps no longer had the VW logo highlighted in black, and the steering wheel lost its semi-circular horn ring in August too.

During 1964 the factory changed its system of chassis numbering, so we have chassis numbers starting at 1-6016121 and ending at 1-6502399 on July 31st, then restarting at 115 000 001 on August 1st. The last chassis number for 1964 is 115 410 000. In August the glass area of the Bug was increased all round, ready for the new model year, the rear window growing 20mm higher and 10mm wider. At the rear, a push-button release replaced the old T-handle on the engine compartment lid. Inside the car, two levers replaced the old turn-knob of the heating control, one opening the heater and the other allowing hot air to vent from under the rear seat. Detail changes to the engine cooling system made for a shorter warm-up period.

For 1965 the chassis numbers started at 115 410 001 and finished at 116 463 103, the third digit, it should be noted, being a reference to the model year (116 = 1966). The most significant introduction that year was the 1300 model, easily identified by the '1300' badge on the rear lid. Wheels were slotted instead of plain, and hubcaps were no longer of the domed type traditionally seen on Beetles. Flat hubcaps similar to those fitted to the Type 3 VW were used. At the front end, the old link-pin and kingpin suspension was replaced by a system using balljoints for both up and down and steering motions. New shock absorbers incorporating bump-stops were used, and stronger rear brake drums were also fitted. With the new engine came a new identification system: D prefix = 1200; E prefix = 1300 (37PS); F prefix = 1300 (40PS).

August 1966 (the year began with chassis number 116 463 104 and finished with 117 442 503) saw the introduction of perhaps the best Beetle ever made – the 1500. This model had a 1500cc engine and disc front brakes. At the rear, wider drums improved efficiency, while a new squared-off engine lid and '1500' badging ensured that the neighbours realized you had bought a new car! Chrome side-trim was narrower than previously and, more significantly, a Z-bar (equalizer) was fitted at the rear to improve handling. The late-style four-bolt wheel was introduced on most models. Doors could be locked without the key thanks to push-down buttons on the door frames.

In 1967 (chassis numbers 117 442 504 to 118 431 603) the most significant changes occurred, as usual, in August ready for the new year. Front and rear lids were shortened, the engine compartment lid especially. The valances at front and rear had thus to be increased in height to accommodate the new lids. The headlamps became 'vertical' using units stolen from the Type 3 range. Bumpers were now of the 'Euro' design, larger and squarer in section than the old rounded type. The trunk lid was fitted with louvers to allow fresh air into the car, and dual-circuit braking was introduced, as were improved safety belt mountings. The fuel gauge was incorporated into the speedometer and two-speed

Front end shape was to remain largely unchanged through the early '60s until the advent of upright headlamps for '68. Window size was increased for '65.

opposite, top
This '51 model is easily identified by its unique vent flaps in the front quarter panels. This was a one-year-only feature to improve ventilation.

opposite, bottom
The first really significant change to the rear end of the Bug was the introduction of the larger window for the '58 model year. Note tail lights.

left
Semaphore turn signals were featured on all Bugs up until the coming of the '60s. They frequently had a mind of their own, as owners will confirm.

below
Rear end remained virtually unchanged from '68 model year through to the last days of the Bug. Vents on deck lid are to allow cooling air to engine.

wipers were fitted. At long last, the 1300 and 1500 Bugs were treated to 12 volt electrics. At the rear, new lights were fitted, with a squared-off bottom edge to match the new rear lid, and for those desirous of an automatic, a semi-auto 'stickshift' model was introduced. This had no clutch pedal, but still needed to be shifted like a manual transmission in all other respects. Perhaps more important was the fact that the stickshift cars had a new rear suspension system consisting of a four-jointed driveshaft set-up and semi-trailing arms. As you can see, 1967 (in readiness for the '68 model year) was an important stage in the Bug's life. VW was becoming aware that the Beetle was an old design.

The year 1968 (chassis numbers 118 431 604 to 119 474 780) saw fewer significant changes than '67, and those that were made were largely for increased security. A cable-operated release was fitted for the fuel filler flap and the handle for the trunk lid release was placed in the glove box. To aid demisting, the fresh air ducts on the dashboard were connected into the heating system.

For '69 (chassis numbers 119 474 781 to 110 2473 153) there were again few major changes. The 1500 Beetle got two sets of louvers in the rear lid for improved engine cooling. The engine itself had a revised oiling system, with two oil-pressure relief valves and enlarged oilways for better circulation. Under the trunk lid a one-piece cover for the dashboard wiring and luggage space could be seen, and wheels became silver painted throughout

The most radical change ever made was when Volkswagen introduced the first of the MacPherson strut Beetles for '71. Note rounded nose.

the range. All these changes happened, inevitably, in August. US-specification cars got an alarm buzzer to remind forgetful drivers that they had left the keys in the ignition. Note that the chassis number now had ten digits.

So to 1970 (chassis numbers 110 2473 154 to 111 2427 591), and in August that year the dual-port cylinder heads arrived on the scene. But that was not all: VW at last made a real effort to bring the Bug into the late twentieth century with the introduction of the 1302 range. These cars, available in 1300cc (1302) and 1600cc (1302S) guises, were a major departure from previous practice, having MacPherson strut front suspension and the four-joint rear suspension incorporating constant velocity joints first seen on stickshift models. To accommodate these changes the floorplan was redesigned – especially at the front end. The trunk lid was also substantially reshaped and this, along with the increased width available as a result of using the new suspension system, gave considerably greater luggage space. The 'original' 1200 and 1300 models continued alongside in a substantially unmodified form.

Incidentally, all engines featuring the new oiling system had identification numbers prefixed with the letter A (AB and AC = 1300cc; AD, AE, AF and AH =

1600cc. Whatever happened to AG?

For 1971 (chassis numbers 111 2427 592 to 112 2427 792) the rear lid developed another pair of louvers in August. Sadly, the water drainage tray behind them was discontinued, guaranteeing hours of fun for owners as they tried to start wet engines! The rear screen was increased in height by 4cm and the steering wheel was changed to a padded type. Other detail changes included a new fuel filler cap and a better ventilation system. Of technical interest was the introduction of a plug-in diagnostic system that allowed garages to monitor the vehicle's electrical functions by simply inserting an electrical connector in a socket located in the engine bay.

In 1972 (chassis numbers 112 2427 793 to 113 2438 833) VW made yet another attempt to bring the Bug up to date with the introduction of the 1303 and 1303S models. The former was equipped with a 1300cc engine, the latter had a 1600cc unit. The new model had a larger 'panoramic' windshield and consequently shortened trunk lid. The dashboard was totally restyled, dropping the bare metal pattern in favour of a deep padded design that would not have looked out of place in a sports car. The rear lights grew enormously in size to cater for new legal requirements across the world. The new model retained the MacPherson strut suspension and even had its own chassis numbering system, commencing on August 1st with 133 2000 001 and

Available with 1300 or 1600 engine, the Super Beetle with its curved windscreen was potentially the best Beetle ever, but it lacks character.

finishing the year on 133 2438 833.

The following year, 1973, (chassis numbers 113 2438 833 to 114 2423 795 and 133 2438 833 to 134 2423 795) saw few changes other than differing trim options to try to capture a few more sales. This was the year when the special models started to appear, such as the denim-upholstered Jeans Beetle, all seemingly desperate attempts by the factory to regain flagging sales, but these seem sadly at odds with the 'honest' nature of the traditional Bug. One good thing to come out of this year was the arrival of the alternator on all larger displacement engines.

In 1974 (chassis numbers 114 2423 796 to 115 2143 743 and 134 2423 796 to 135 2143 743) the Beetle range was reduced, and indeed on July 1st the very last Beetle rolled off the production line at Wolfsburg, the Bug's home since the day it was born. With 11,916,519 cars built since 1945, the end was in sight for the Bug. It was no coincidence that production of the Golf and Scirocco water-cooled models was getting under way . . .

All models from August on were fitted with indicators mounted in the front bumpers, ideally placed for maximum damage in a minor accident! The rear valance was enlarged to accomodate the catalytic converter now

required in the USA. A fuel-injected version was introduced for the US market, with just one tailpipe giving the game away when the car was viewed from the rear. For a strange reason, the 'S' suffix was dropped from the badging on the rear of the 1303S models. Rack and pinion steering was introduced on 1303 and Cabriolet models from chassis number 135 2000 001.

In 1975 (chassis numbers 115 2143 743 to 116 2071 467 and 135 2143 743 to 135 2600 000 – note that the latter is the last chassis number for July 31st for reasons that will become immediately obvious!), big things were to happen. Volkswagen decided to kill off the 1303 models, allowing them to continue only in Cabriolet form, built by the Karmann factory. The Cabriolets had their own chassis numbering system starting at 156 2000 001 on August 1st and finishing on 156 2071 467 at the end of the year. The basic Bug continued with either 1200cc or 1600cc engine options.

In 1976 (chassis numbers 116 2071 468 to 117 2063 700 and 156 2071 468 to 157 2063 700 for the Cabrios) no changes took place to the specification of the Bug other than a revision of the trim options and colors, etc.

The same held true for the year 1977 (chassis numbers 117 2063 701 to 118 2050 000 and from 157 2063 701 to 158 2028 542 for the Cabrios) but, alas, the Bug was axed from US dealers' line-up.

In 1978 (chassis numbers 118 2100 001 to 119 2108 687

Volkswagen tried many gimmicks to improve flagging sales – the Jeans Beetle was one of them. Interior featured denim-look upholstery on seats.

and 158 2100 000 to 159 2018 069 for the Cabrios) there were no major changes to the remains of the Beetle range. Production in Germany finally ceased, leaving VW's factory in Mexico to produce Bugs for the European market. The models were unsophisticated, with torsion bar front suspension and swing-axle rear. Engines were just 1200cc in capacity, except for the Cabrio which continued with the larger engine and still came out of the Karmann factory in Germany.

For 1979 (chassis numbers 119 2108 688 to 119 2150 000 – until July 31st – and 11A 000 001 to 11A 008 929 for the rest of the year, Cabrios 159 2018 070 to 159 2043 634) there were again no major changes to the seemingly unloved Bug.

The next year saw the demise of the Cabrio on January 10th 1980. The chassis number was 152 044 140, but don't expect to find it for sale – it's in the Karmann museum in Osnabrück. No other changes were made to the Bug range, such as it was. Chassis numbers began at 11A 008 930 and finished the model year (July 31st) on 11A 0020 000. Mexican numbering is very different to the old system used by Germany as you can see.

From this point on the Bug has drifted aimlessly through time, with changes being made here and there solely to trim and paintwork. The Bug continues to be manufactured in South America but without the quality and desirability of the good old German cars. Perhaps it is best if we simply relate the chassis numbers available up to the end of the 1985 model year and then let the Bug rest quietly in peace.

For what was once such a proud car, a real struggler against all odds, it seems a shame that the last years appear little more than a prolonging of the inevitable agony. If only the German factory had not given up production, and if only the danger signals had been read earlier on in the Bug's life when more modern rivals came on the scene. All the attempts by the factory to rekindle interest in the Bug seemed so half-hearted. But then 'if only' are two very easy words to say in hindsight.

Chassis numbers were
1981 model year:
11B 000 001 to 11B 013 340,
1982 model year
11C 000 001 to 11C 009 836,
1983 model year
11D 000 001 to 11D 017 323,
1984 model year
11E 000 001 to 11E 020 000,
1985 model year
11F 000 001 to 11F 020 000.

GT Beetle gave the impression that sporting changes had been made to the slow old Bug, but it was all show and no go! This race driver is an optimist.

BUYING YOUR BUG

Don't let your heart rule your head

So you want to buy your first Beetle? That's great, but remember, there are quite a few things to consider before parting with your hard-earned money. It can be quite a minefield out there, so let's take a look at what you should and shouldn't do, and what to look for when you think you've found the car of your dreams.

There are several ways of running to earth a Beetle for sale: your local newspaper, the classified columns of your favorite car magazine, the national autotrader publications, your local used car dealer, word of mouth, through a club, at a show or . . . Well, as you can see, the possibilities are almost endless.

However, before you actually start looking for a Beetle to buy, the first thing you have to do is decide exactly how much you are prepared to pay. That may seem an obvious thing to say, but it saves you from coming away disappointed when that VW Cabriolet you saw turns out to cost more than you earn in a year.

Be sensible when setting a budget. Every used car is going to need some money spent on it unless you happen to buy from a reputable dealer who is offering a trustworthy warranty – and with any Beetle now being relatively old, the chances of that are pretty slim. Always endeavor to leave some sort of financial buffer when buying just in case the car proves not to be as good as you first thought. It happens, and more frequently than many would care to admit.

The next thing to do is decide on what sort of Beetle you would like, or rather what type you do not want. Do you prefer the idea of running a sound early car which, despite poor lights, almost no heating and seemingly a total lack of power, has masses of character and will possibly increase in value if you look after it? Or does the idea of sophisticated (in Beetle terms!) ventilation, MacPherson strut suspension, disc brakes and a heater that actually demists the windows sound more like

heaven to you? Perhaps, then, that 1303S 'Super Beetle' is just the buy. Or what about that semi-automatic 'Stickshift' Beetle that is going cheap in the local newspaper? It may be rust-free and low mileage, but can you accept the slightly idiosyncratic clutchless gearchange and reduced performance?

These are the kinds of question you have to ask yourself. In most cases the answer will come back: 'I just want a Beetle – the best I can afford!' So be it, but be warned, you may not make the right choice first time out. We have all been guilty of buying the first car that comes along because we were too anxious to own a legend. Try to be patient, but failing that, do at least remember to keep within your financial limitations.

There in the driveway of the seller's house sits this Beetle – it's a tidy looking '66, and the price seems right. At least, that is what your friends say and they all own Beetles. So where do you start? The general rules are the same for most VWs, so we'll talk in generalities for the moment.

Chances are that the fenders will have been damaged at some time in the car's life. It happens all too easily, although heaven knows why, for the Beetle really is quite compact and there are not many modern cars which offer better visibility. Still, fenders are the least of your worries, being easily replaceable and relatively inexpensive. No, the first thing you want to cast an eye over is that panel between the door and the rear fender – are there signs of rust along the bottom of it? Rot here is indicative of two things: that the wheel arch has rotted through in front of the rear wheels, allowing water into the rocker panels (sills), and that you are soon going to be in for some expense putting it right. Rust in this area is very common and unfailingly destructive if left to its own devices. It gets into the rocker panels, heater channels and eventually the floorpan as water enters the car.

left
If you have your heart set on a Karmann-bodied cabriolet, then expect to pay a lot more than you would for an equivalent sedan version of the Bug.

above
Most Bugs you see for sale are offered privately. This sad example is a well-worn workhorse that has seen better days. But it may be a good buy.

Every first-timer dreams of owning a beauty like this, but these days it is becoming increasingly hard to find good clean early Beetles for sale.

Try to look down between the running boards and rocker panels for signs of the outer panel rusting through. Waggle the running board and listen for sounds of crumbling metal if necessary. Don't be put off by the owner trying to stop you pulling his car apart. It's your money that is going to change hands, not his.

Look under the front fender behind the wheel. Once again, rust is very common here and can lead to water entering the heater channels from the front. More expense if not put right soon. While looking under the front, get right down and, with a flashlight, check the condition of the front bulkhead. It is not easy to see properly, but check it all the same. Corrosion can lead to a damp interior at best, but an expensive welding bill is more likely. It is a tricky panel to repair so be warned.

The spare wheel well is another common weak point on older cars. Lift out the spare and check inside the front valance. If you can see the road, do not despair but use it as a bargaining point should you eventually decide to buy the car. Now, while you have the trunk lid open, take a close look at the condition of the rubber seal round the edge of the bodywork. Once again, chances are that the seal is broken and set in the rotten remains of what used to be a small channel welded round the trunk opening. Just poke around and ascertain whether the rust has gone all the way through or not. If it's limited to surface rust then all is well, but anything worse can lead to another large repair bill.

At the back end of the car, look at the rear bumper mountings. This area is prone to rust as dirt from the rear tires is thrown up and sticks there like glue. Not an expensive panel to replace but again a good bargaining point. Check too the condition of the body mounting panel adjacent to the tops of the rear shock absorbers – this corrodes and then cracks as suspension stresses cause the panel to flex.

Open up the doors – do they open smoothly or have the hinges seized? Now run your fingers along the bottom of each door. Is there any rust here and if so does it go all the way through? Bad rust can eat its way out through the skin of the door as a result of blocked drainage channels allowing water to sit inside the doors. Pull off the interior door panel if you can and use a flashlight to look inside. If all you see is nice clean paint then fine, but chances are that reality will be in the form of accumulations of large flakes of rust. Not a pretty sight.

Now is the time to look at the bottoms of the door pillars below where the lower hinges are fixed. A gaping hole here is indicative of plenty of expense and probably ruined rocker panels too as water has breached the defenses somewhere. Look also under the carpet by the footwell and see if the floor is wet and the heater channel rotten. It probably will be on any car that is showing signs of neglect elsewhere.

Lift up the rear seat squab and take a good hard look at the state of the body down in the corners near the heater

When you begin to look for your first Beetle, remember that they come in all shapes and colors! Visiting a VW show may be the best way to start.

'Closer examination reveals plenty of accident damage to the front end. Quarter panel will need replacing along with the fender and trunk lid.

Tell-tale rust along the bottoms of the doors needs repair. Note too rust on the quarter panel and rear fender.

This is why it pays to look closely at the rocker panels behind the running boards. Rust has taken hold and now allows water to enter the car.

In the trunk you should check for signs of corrosion behind the spare wheel. This Bug will need a lot of costly repair

left
From the rear the Bug does not look so bad, but the missing tailpipe will hurt performance. Check out damage to left rear fender.

above right
Some models of Bug were fitted with this neat shield under the deck lid to prevent water getting into the engine bay. A useful addition.

below right
Models that had vented lids but no shielding above the engine are prone to starting problems in wet weather. Note how the engine is exposed to rain.

BUYING YOUR BUG

channels (by the regulator on later cars). Once again, and I don't mean to be the bearer of bad tidings all the time, you have to expect signs of corrosion here. It just happens! It must be repaired soon or things will start to get out of hand. Lift up the carpet under the rear window and look for signs of rust on the floor of the luggage area behind the rear seat. This will point to a leaky rear window seal, a common problem on cars that have been resprayed and the drain holes left blocked with paint.

One final check while you have the door open and the rear seat up – look under the battery. This is another favorite trouble area as battery acid eats its way through precious metal. It also happens to be the lowest point on the floorpan so any water that has crept in through other problem areas tends to find its way here to add to the headache.

Less serious rust may also be found in the lip around the front edge of the trunk lid and similarly round the bottom of the engine cover. It is hardly likely to affect the structural integrity of the car but will make the vehicle look less appealing than it otherwise might.

Fenders? Well, if you are unlucky they can rust through around the headlight and even where the running boards bolt on, but apart from that, parking damage is all you need think about.

So what now? You have established that the only rust on the Bug of your dreams is easily repairable by the Mr Fixit who lives next door, and you can live with the fenders for a few more months. But what about those spots of oil on the driveway under the back of the car?

First thing to remember when buying a Beetle is take no notice whatsoever of the mileometer. The chances are that if the mileage appears low, the car has been 'round the clock' at least once, and if the mileage is high than you can be sure that the true mileage is even higher! Beetles can cover huge mileages without problem, but in everyday use and at the hands of more than a few owners they do tend to suffer from age like the rest of us.

Start the engine. It shouldn't need more than a few turns before firing up. It it cranks over slowly then it could be a low battery (poor charging system? Bad earth?) or a faulty starter looking for someone to quit on. If the car is a pre-'67 then it could just be a case of a good old six volt electrical system doing its natural thing – being lazy! If the engine fires and idles straight away without drama then try revving it up a bit and watch for tell-tale signs of smoke from the tailpipes, which could point to worn piston rings or valve guides. A slight piston slap when cold is acceptable, but this should disappear quickly as the engine warms up.

Listen for dull knocking sounds from the bottom end of the engine. If they are fast and regular then the cam followers could be on the way out. Deeper rumblings point to worn main bearings, while a very unhealthy knock may turn out to be worn big-ends. Any of these will mean splitting the engine open and spending money. Unless you are prepared to get involved in buying reconditioned engines or repairing a worn one yourself, leave such a car alone.

Any Beetle with over 60,000 miles on the clock (the true clock that is, not the fairy-tale one fitted in the dash!) will be due for a top-end overhaul soon – at the very least exhaust valves and guides, a full decoke, valve grind and possibly a new set of piston rings into the bargain. The valve gear will also be worn on a higher mileage engine,

resulting in clattery rocker arms and noisy tappets despite constant adjustment.

Oil leaks are almost part and parcel of VW ownership – rather like the good old British motorcycles of days gone by. Common 'moist' areas are around the pushrod tubes, from within the fan-shrouding (could be a leaky oil-cooler?), around the base of the cylinder barrels, from the oil pump, from behind the crankshaft pulley (worn pulley or did someone leave out the oil thrower ring when doing a home rebuild?) or, worst of all, from the bellhousing area of the transmission, pointing to a leaking rear main oil seal. The latter will require removal of the engine and flywheel and almost certain replacement of the clutch assembly due to oil contamination.

If an engine looks black and sticky all over the underside, treat it as an item to be replaced forthwith. If the outside is a total mess, the possibilities of the same being true of the inside are high. Look inside the oil filler cap to confirm your worst suspicions. If the oil is black and foamy then the car has probably only been used for short journeys, allowing moisture to build up in the crankcase. This can mean that the engine has never had a chance to warm up properly before being used in heavy traffic – not good for any internal combustion engine.

Try selecting each gear in turn and gently easing out the clutch pedal. Does the car try to move away? Good – at least you have got all four forward gears, and hopefully reverse too! How does that clutch feel? Is there a lot of free play in the pedal? That could mean that the cable is on the way out, or that the assembly simply requires readjustment. It could also indicate a well-worn centerplate.

Push hard on the brake pedal – it should go down about an inch before becoming firm. If you can push it all the way to the floor you have problems! They could be caused by air in the brake circuit, or by worn master cylinder or wheel cylinders. It could be that the flexible brake pipes are on the way out and actually ballooning under pressure. Think twice before taking this car out.

Waggle the steering wheel from side to side while a friend holds one of the front wheels. Is there excessive play in the steering box? The steering wheel should only move about an inch at the rim if all is perfect. With the wheel turned on full lock you will be able to detect a lot more play in the steering, such is the design of VW steering boxes. With this in mind, always check the steering free play with the wheels in the dead-ahead position.

Get out of the car and take hold of the front wheels one at a time. Try shaking them from the top to check for wear in the ball-joints ('65-on models) or kingpins (earlier cars). Shake them from side to side to check for wear in the wheel bearings and tie-rod ends.

Take a good look at the condition of the tires. Uneven wear on front tires suggests that the steering is out of alignment. Is it due to wear of components or has the car been involved in an accident at some time in its past? Are the tires in good condition overall, with plenty of tread left on them? Are the sidewalls cracked and perished? Are the tires a matched set? Ask yourself all these questions and note any defects for future bargaining.

Bounce the car up and down at each corner to check

If the engine is clean and oil-tight like this appears to be, then it is a good indication of condition. Note aftermarket carburetor on this Bug.

for damper wear. The vehicle should rebound just once when you push down hard on the fenders. If it continues to bob up and down for a while then reckon on investing in new dampers. This is especially important on Super Beetles, as MacPherson strut units are considerably more costly to replace.

Sitting back inside the car once more, take a good look at the overall condition of the upholstery – it can often tell you more about how the vehicle has been treated in its previous life than any other area. Worn and torn seats suggest hard use, high mileage and owners who haven't been too particular in their use of the Bug. Worn carpets are a sure sign of much use, as are severely worn pedal rubbers. Headlinings are frequently discolored especially if the owner smokes a lot of cigarettes. Torn headlinings are unsightly and difficult for the inexperienced owner to replace.

OK, so it's drive time! Crank over the engine, fasten your seat belt and take her for a spin. Check the gear change, brakes (do they pull to one side or the other?), steering (is it stiff, or sloppy?) and clutch (does it judder when you pull away?). Listen out for whines from the

transmission, clunks from CV joints on later cars, jumping out of gear when decelerating, and expensive sounding noises from the engine!

Does the engine pull well? Don't expect a humble 1200 Bug to be a freeway flier, but it ought to deliver respectable performance without feeling tired and sluggish. A 1500 or 1600 version should pull well and feel a whole lot more powerful than the smaller versions but late-model cars often suffer from flat-spots in the carburation, making the vehicle hesitate momentarily when accelerating.

If you feel happy with the Bug, and remember, no vehicle of this age is going to be perfect unless it has been the subject of a 100-point restoration, then decide whether the price is what you can afford, the defects can be put right without going over budget and that you really do want a Bug! But be warned – buy your first VW and you'll find yourself hooked for life. Good hunting!

SAVED FROM THE GRAVE

There's hope yet for that rotted out Bug!

As you will have realized by now, the Volkswagen Beetle, despite a legendary reputation for long life and resistance to rot, suffers just like every other car on the road from corrosion. Indeed, while it may be true that Bugs last a little longer than most rivals, when they do rot it can be on a major scale. But this need not concern you too much if you have access to repair facilities or a good body repair shop, for there is hardly a body repair panel that is not available for the average Bug. Certainly you might have a few problems finding some of the unique panels used on early models (do you know where you can buy a new front quarter panel for a '51?), but in general the vehicle is well served by a whole host of companies marketing new parts.

The chapter on buying a Bug gives you a pretty good idea of where to expect trouble on the rust front, but to briefly recap, the main problem areas tend to be the rocker panels (sills), front and rear inner fenders and bumper mountings, spare wheel well, under the rear seat and the rear quarter panels. Saying it like that makes it seem as if there wouldn't be much left of your Bug if you cut out all the rust!

Disassembly of the VW ready for major body repair is relatively straightforward, requiring only basic handtools, although access to an air-chisel would be useful to save time. You will need plenty of space around the car as there is nothing worse than trying to work on a Beetle with no room to open the doors wide. Only by doing so will you be able to effectively carry out repairs to the rocker panels and interior.

Let us follow through the repair work carried out on a fairly typical early 1970s Beetle by the House of Haselock in England. The car was bought having been offered for sale at the side of the road. It was a basic 1200 model in orange with white interior, and apart from slightly untidy fenders appeared to be sound. Especially good were the bottoms of the door pillars and the rear quarter panels. The asking price was fair for a car of this vintage, so money changed hands and restoration began.

Preliminary work involved stripping the car of its fenders and running boards to give access to the potential problem areas of rocker panels and front and rear inner arches. To remove the fenders you will need a 14mm socket or wrench and some patience. The major problem with removing fenders from an old car is that the captive nuts into which the mounting bolts screw frequently become rusted and tear out of the body when you try to undo the bolts. Similarly the running boards, which are retained with a series of 10mm-headed bolts, can lead to much frustration as captive nuts pull out of the

rocker panel. In really bad cases you can simply take hold of the running board and pull hard!

Do not despair when the captive nuts pull out of the bodywork as it is possible to buy replacement ones which can be welded back in place. Use a long 8mm bolt to hold the new nut when tack welding it into position. Run an 8mm tap through all the other existing captive nuts. It will be a joy to refit the fenders with all new, or at least all good, mountings.

Some Bugs are just a little too far gone! Even the skills of the best bodyshop in the world would be hard-pressed to bring this Beetle back!

above right
If the fender bolts break or tear out, don't despair for you can buy new captive nuts to weld into the quarter panel. The nut is held with a long bolt – but don't forget it will get hot when welding! Use vice-grips.

right
You can see the corrosion here in the spare wheel well. Repair of this area is not difficult as all the panels are readily available across the counter of your local VW specialist. Remove bumper prior to further work.

With the fenders out of the way you get a far clearer picture of the condition of your Bug – indeed it's a pity that you can't take them off before buying a car as it would give a far clearer indication of the overall condition. Not surprisingly this idea might not have the same appeal to a potential vendor.

Taking a screwdriver, we poked hard at the rocker panels and inner fender panels. The likelihood of these panels being totally rust free on a Bug these days is pretty remote unless you happen to live in California or Arizona. For the rest of us, reality is a screwdriver disappearing through paper-thin metal to leave behind a large hole in a panel that originally looked sound.

Opening the trunk lid and taking out the spare wheel on 'our' car showed the front end to be rusted out in the usual places – spare wheel well, the bulkhead panel in front of the fuel tank, bumper mountings, etc. – but this was to be expected as the initial inspection at the time of purchase had confirmed it as a 'bargaining point'.

The bottom edges of the front inner fenders were a little ragged and would benefit from a repair panel being inserted, while the rocker panels themselves were particularly bad at the front end. This is why the floor was slightly damp inside when we lifted the rubber mats. At the rear, the body mounting panels were rusted on both sides, while the bumper mountings had all but disappeared. The rear valance was at least intact and straight.

Taking a look inside the car with the interior trim completely stripped out – again a worthwhile step if you

A Beetle deserves to have absolutely flawless bodywork like this — the shape is so pure and simple that every blemish will stand out a mile.

have any internal work to do – it soon became obvious that this Bug, although superficially sound, was to need a fair amount of repair work to the rear wheel arch area on both sides and to the panel above the torsion bar assembly.

At least the doors, pillars, rear quarters and floorpan were sound!

Starting at the front end, the first job was to remove the fuel tank and the trunk lid. Although the latter did not require repair, access was greatly improved. The fuel tank should always be removed whenever any welding is carried out at the front of the car, for obvious safety reasons. All it takes is one stray spark and a small fuel leak . . .

To remove the tank, get underneath the car and clamp the flexible fuel line where it exits the tank. Pull the connection off the chassis and block the line with a rubber dust cap from a brake bleed nipple. Up above, you'll need to undo the four retaining bolts round the edge of the tank and, if it's a later model with an external fuel filler assembly, loosen the hoses to the filler and breather. It's wise to get help from a friend to lift the tank out as it's quite awkward and can be heavy if there's any fuel left in it.

Removal of the tank gives you free access to check the condition of the bulkhead by the master cylinder – in our case we were lucky, but other cars might not be so good. This is also an ideal time to take a look at the steering damper, brake pipes and steering coupling – all parts which are more easily viewed with the tank out of the way.

Remove the front bumper by undoing the bolts located either side of the spare wheel well (or under the wheel arch on later cars) and then ascertain exactly the extent of the rust to be repaired. In this instance, rot was more extensive than we first thought so it was necessary to cut right back as far as the fuel tank mountings. The entire front end sheet metal was cut away with an air-chisel and then discarded as one piece. It looked drastic, but would prove to be the easiest solution in the long run.

There are several panels available to carry out a full repair on the front of your Bug, and it seemed we needed them all. Basically it proved necessary to replace the panel behind the spare wheel, the two front bumper mounting panels (which also form the sides of the spare wheel well), the bottom of the spare wheel well and the front valance. The first thing to do is to check the panels closely for fit by offering them up against the trimmed

above
Any major bodywork session that involves welding should commence with removal of the fuel tank. It is located by four bolts around the edge. You must also loosen the fittings to the fuel filler assembly as shown.

above right
This particular Beetle was very badly rotted and it was considered necessary to cut off the entire front of the car from the fuel tank forwards. Using a 'nibbler' the cut is easy. You can use an air-chisel.

right
Be very careful not to cut yourself on the sharp edges exposed after major surgery like this. Removing the front panels in one piece like this saves a lot of time in the long run. Clean up the jagged edges.

48

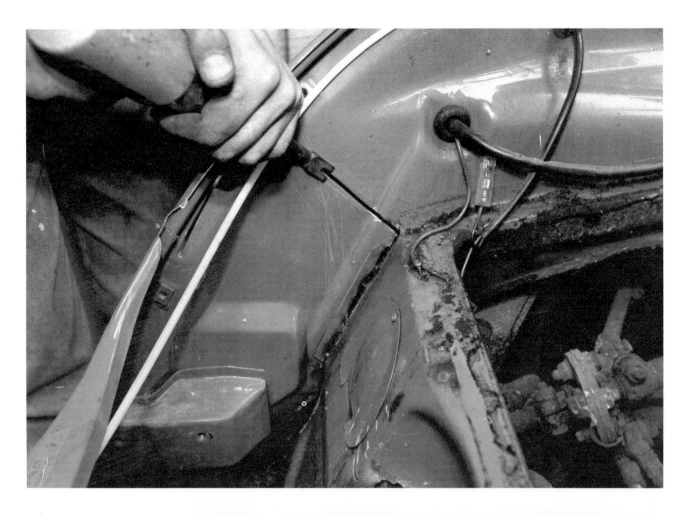

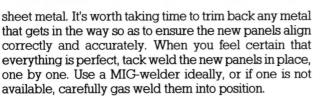

sheet metal. It's worth taking time to trim back any metal that gets in the way so as to ensure the new panels align correctly and accurately. When you feel certain that everything is perfect, tack weld the new panels in place, one by one. Use a MIG-welder ideally, or if one is not available, carefully gas weld them into position.

Stand back from the car every now and then and check by eye that everything is in line. It could be that the car has been in an accident at some time, but that the damage isn't obvious. Take a steel rule and measure from a few reference points as well. Only when you are certain that the panels are aligned correctly should you weld them into place.

Taking a look at the rocker panels, we could see that the front end was badly rusted out although the heater channel inside the car was sound. The remainder of the panel appeared to be good, but a little work with a screwdriver soon revealed more corrosion than first thought. This is often the way with Bugs – they look sound on the outside, but a close inspection soon reveals that all is not what it seems.

Using an air-chisel, the remains of the rocker panel were cut out in readiness for a new set of panels. These consisted of an outer panel, another to repair the underside along by the floorpan and a special reinforcing panel to go under the jacking point. The

opposite, top
The Bug was repaired using five separate pressings – bulkhead, spare wheel well, two quarter panels and a front apron. This is all rather like doing a jigsaw puzzle and you need to take care to align everything.

opposite, bottom
With the alignment to your satisfaction, you can break out the MIG-welder and begin to tack the panels into place. Only when you are absolutely sure that everything is in line do you complete the welding.

above left
The correct way to repair a rusted rocker panel is to cut out the old panel with an air-chisel. Leave the top side of panel intact as the new one will fit over the top for extra strength.

above right
The stock jacking points leave a lot to be desired as they frequently give way when you least expect (or need!) it. Haselock's make this repair/strengthening panel to weld in behind the stock jacking point.

latter is not a standard factory part, but is recommended when repairs have been made to the rocker panel as it gives a lot of strength to this important area.

The main repair panel was designed to slip over the top of the upper part of the rocker panel where the door opening is. This facilitates fitting by ensuring that there is something solid to use as a reference point when starting to weld. Most repair panels are 'user friendly', to steal a computing term, and designed for ease of fitting.

At the front, the inner wheel arch was very 'soft' – a polite expression for being rotted out. The rust that had started in the rocker panel had spread up though the inner fender panel, meaning that there was only one course of action. The air-chisel was brought into play again and used to cut out all traces of corrosion prior to offering up the repair panel. This is a very staightforward part to fit and is almost guaranteed to make your Bug waterproof.

The rear of the car was a mess – at least it looked that way once the body shop had got hold of it. The first job to do was strip off all the underseal that had been applied in a desperate attempt to keep rust at bay. This revealed (doesn't it always?) that the bumper mountings and body mounting panel required replacement on both sides of the Bug.

The bumper mounting panel is a frequent candidate for repair as it collects all the dirt thrown up by the back

above
Here is the new rocker panel being offered up to the Bug. Notice how the top laps over the original panel? Notice too the drainage holes pre-drilled in the new panel, the sign of a good quality repair panel.

below
Under the front fenders you will frequently discover that the panel behind the wheel needs replacement as rot has set in. The best course of action is to cut the old metal right back and replace with a new panel.

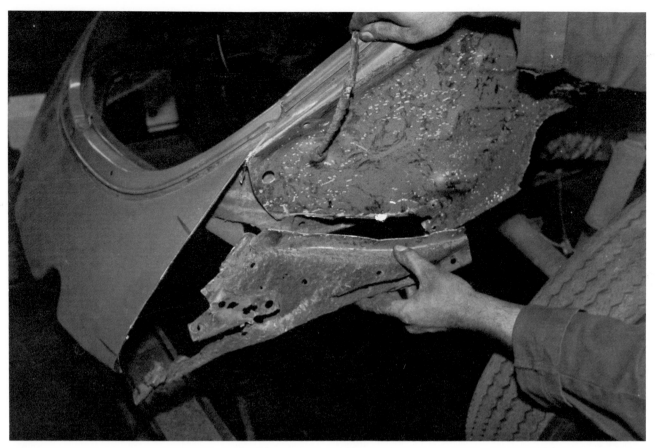

above
The rear bumper mountings almost always need replacement on an older Beetle. You can see here that the panel has been eaten away by rust very badly. Cutting it out as shown left the rear apron intact on our Bug.

below
The repair panel is a lot larger than you will probably need, but does allow you to cut to the exact size. Lip on edge slips behind the rear apron. Note the bolt holes supplied ready for the new fender to mount.

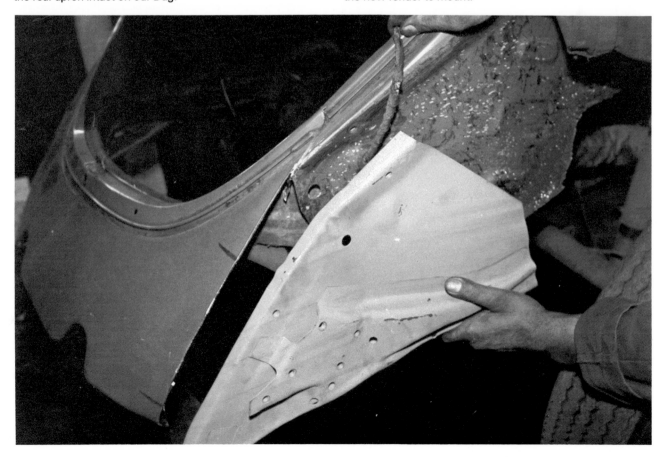

tires. Removal is straightforward and replacement likewise thanks to the availability of large repair panels which have plenty of extra metal to allow for trimming to size. If you need to replace the rear valance at the same time, then take care to ensure that the alignment of the panels is correct. The easiest way to check this is to bolt up the new fenders and use them as reference points to align the valance. Once that is established then you can confidently weld in the bumper repair panels.

The body mounting panel also carries the Z-bar stabilizer (if fitted) and this will have to be unbolted first if you are to carry out an effective repair. The body mounting panel is reinforced here and you can clearly see the area that needs to be cut out – just follow the edge of the reinforcement. The new panel is a lot larger and allows for some additional strengthening of the area. As a reference point for location, you can fix the new panel to the chassis using the body mounting bolt just in front of the damper mount. This shows you the exact positioning of the new panel.

Turning our attention to the interior of the car, removal of the rear seat and carpet revealed that there was extensive rust of the wheel arch area from inside. Although small repair panels are available for this area, the corrosion on 'our' Bug was too great so it was necessary to fabricate a repair panel to suit. On one side of the car it was necessary to make three separate panels to effect a satisfactory repair.

When you have carried out any repair work of this nature, it is vital to cover the new panels and welds with a rust preventative coating to stop further corrosion. Nothing rusts quicker than new, unprotected, metal. It is a matter of some debate whether conventional underseals are a good thing or not. Placing a rubberized coating over the underside of your car would seem to be a good idea, but many people think this actually encourages rust, for once the protective coating is

above
Corrosion of the rear body mounting under the fender is another common problem. Frequently it gets so bad that the only course open is to cut out the entire area. Note that you will have to remove stabilizer bar.

top right
This is the new body mounting panel – doesn't that look better already? Note the mountings for the stabilizer bar to the left, and body mounting bracket to the right. You must remove interior trim before welding.

bottom right
Access to a professional spray-booth would be great, but many show-winning Beetles have been sprayed in a regular workshop.

punctured by a stone, water is free to seep in and spread between the underseal and the metal work. Growing in popularity these days are spray-on wax and oil protective coatings which can also be injected into body cavities for protection from the inside. The beauty of these coatings is that they are self-sealing in the event of stone chipping and very easy to apply, if a little messy at first.

A number of repair specialists will zinc spray the underside of fenders or stove enamel them to help prevent damage from stone chips and the onset of corrosion. Let's face it, if you have invested your life savings in buying and restoring a Bug, then it pays to protect your investment.

All this should not serve to put you off the idea of buying a Beetle – far from it. If anything it should encourage you, as it goes to prove that, no matter how desperate things appear to be, the chances are that a repair can be made without too much fuss. That is the beauty of the Bug – there is so much available to keep it going.

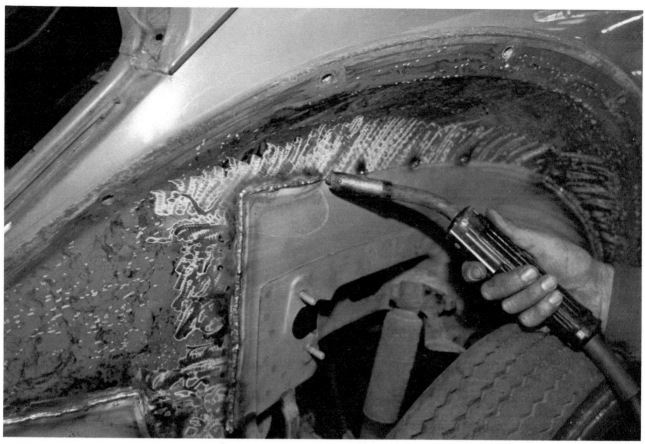

above
Because of the strength needed in this panel, it is best to run a seam weld all the way along the edge rather than just tack it every inch or so. To avoid distortion, use a MIG-welder like this if at all possible.

below
Inside the car you will probably have to repair the area under and behind the rear seat. In the vast majority of cases it will be necessary to make up a new panel out of sheet metal as shown here. Neat job!

above
All ready for the spray shop! Photographer Mike Key carried out the restoration of this Bug for his daughter working in his garage at home. The car is already in primer and just waiting for final coats.

below
To protect your new investment, Haselock's recommend having the underside of the fenders stove enamelled. This protects them from stone chips and also makes it a lot easier to keep them clean. A neat finishing touch.

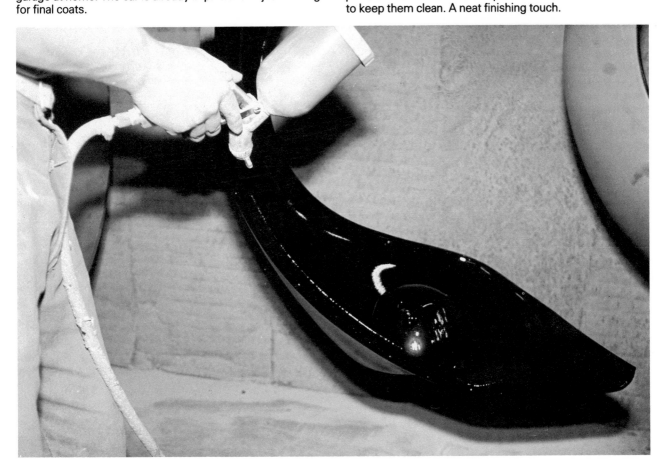

SO COOL, SO CAL
The lowdown on California Look

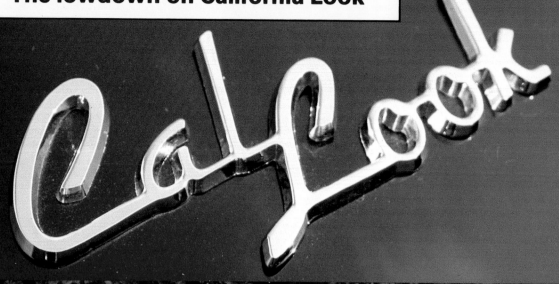

The magazine that started a trend! The February 1975 issue of *Dune Buggies and Hot VWs* saw the first references to the term California Look.

The roots of the California Look lie with the early drag race Beetles with their lowered front ends, hot engines and lack of chrome trim.

The term California Look, or Cal Look for short, has slipped into VW parlance almost unchallenged, being the accepted term for almost any air-cooled Volkswagen that has been lowered, had its side-chrome removed and been repainted in an eye catching color. But Cal Look goes much further than that, and it is worth taking a look back at its roots to see why.

Before February 1975, the expression California Look was unknown, for it was in that month's issue of the American magazine *Dune Buggies and Hot VWs* that the style was first given the recognition it deserved. In reality you have to go back much further still.

It was way back in 1956 that the California Look saga really began, for it was in that year that EMPI, the famed VW tuning company, was first formed, though you wouldn't find any exotic tuning equipment in a glossy catalog back then. No, the first EMPI products were replacement valve guides, enabling worn VW heads to be salvaged. Gradually thoughts turned towards hopping up the humble flat four in search of some extra horses, such thinking leading to the famous victory in the Bahamas Grand Prix in 1962 by Dan Gurney driving an EMPI-prepared Bug, 'Inch Pincher'. This same Bug went on to become perhaps the most famous VW drag race car of all time. being raced successfully against much larger machinery by Dean Lowry and Darrell Vittone, son of EMPI founder Joe Vittone.

The race exploits of this Bug inspired a growing number of fans to start messing with their own VWs, resulting in the formation of Der Kleiner Panzers, a performance-oriented VW club led by one Ron Fleming. In 1966, DKP were responsible for the first ever VW-only drag race meeting in history, held at Carlsbad Raceway in California.

The popular look at the time was a clean paint job, chrome wheels, Goodyear Blue Streak tires, no bumpers, Weber-carbed motor and a stock – or even slightly raised – ride height. It was club member Greg Aronson who bought himself a '63 Sedan with which he created the first ever California Look car as we know the style today. Aronson treated the Bug to a plain white paint job, bolted a set of EMPI-BRM mag alloy wheels shod with Pirelli tires, and built a hot Webered motor to slip in the back. Perhaps even more significantly, he had a local VW bodyshop weld up all the holes left by removing the trim and then lowered the front end with a Select-A-Drop lowering device. The Calfornia Look was all but complete.

Aronson sold the white Bug after a while to a guy called Jim Holmes, having removed the hot motor and trick transmission. After a while, Holmes returned to Fleming and Aronson to have them build what was to become the archetypal Cal Look motor for many years: 88mm barrels and pistons to give a nominal 1700cc, Engle 110 camshaft, Bosch 009 distributor and a pair of huge 48IDA Weber carbureters. Although such an induction system is considered by many to be overkill today, back in the early seventies you just had to have dual 48s on the street!

A significant legal change came into force around this time, with Californian law requiring every car to be fitted with bumpers of some kind. With the very essence of Cal Look being the removal of such excess material, attentions turned to the nerf bar as a means of getting round the law while still retaining the clean, lean look.

As happens with all such local trends – and being almost exclusively limited at the time to the Orange County area of Los Angeles, it was very local – it took a little while for the media to catch on to what was happening. But in early '75 *Hot VWs* magazine did just that. Jere Alhadeff, VW enthusiast and journalist, identified what was happening out there and produced a piece for the magazine with features on four cars, one being Jim Holmes's ex-Aronson Looker. It is Alhadeff that gets the credit for coining the term California Look, and it is therefore him and the likes of Greg Aronson we thank today for helping create what must be the most tasteful form of VW customizing ever seen.

Creating a Cal Looker – or what passes for one today – is perhaps the easiest of conversions to carry out but it could also be one of the most involved, for there are now so many variations on the basic theme that it is only the size of the owner's imagination and wallet that limit things. But let's take a look at the basic principles.

The most popular Bugs to use for Cal Look styling are the models fitted with torsion-bar front suspension, especially pre- '65ers with their cute rounded form and smaller windows.

The starting point is a healthy lowering job all round. This process is covered in detail in the chapter on suspension and handling, but it's worth mentioning here in outline. Basically the front suspension can be lowered by a variety of means, the most popular these days being the torsion bar adjusters, or Sway-A-Ways as they are often called (Sway-A-Way is in fact the name of a company that manufactures suspension components for VWs). These have to be welded into the center of a torsion bar assembly, replacing the standard factory torsion leaf locating bolts. You can either fit an adjuster to just one torsion bar tube, or a pair, one to each. With two fitted, it is possible to achieve very radical degrees of lowering – as much as five or six inches in extreme cases, although such modifications will require attention to tie-rod ends and balljoints.

The problem with the latter is that balljoints have a limited angle of movement – dropping the suspension too far can cause a balljoint to reach its maximum angle, in effect 'bottoming out' the joint. This is particularly a problem on the Bug's sister, the Type 3, where the design of the suspension allows for radical lowering without recourse to Sway-A-Way adjusters and such like. The simple answer is not to lower too radically if a lot of street driving is envisaged.

Other methods of lowering include cutting the torsion tubes either side of the central locating bolts, turning and then rewelding so that the angle of the trailing arms is altered. The problem with this is that there is no chance of adjusting the ride height once the operation is complete – save by cutting and welding once more. Note also that you can use a Select-A-Drop, an older and less satisfactory weld-on lowering device that effectively pulls one set of torsion leaves round against the other. Alternatively there is the bolt-on Select-A-Drop which, as the name implies, is a device that requires no cutting or welding, but sadly does not allow a very great degree of lowering.

At the rear, and again this will be covered in detail in

This is how you get the front of your Cal Looker down and still retain a good ride. A pair of torsion bar adjusters have been welded into the beam.

the suspension chapter, you can drop the suspension by removing and turning the spring plates which are located on splines on the outer ends of the rear torsion bars. You could instead fit adjustable spring plates, which allow for an infinite range of adjustment by the turn of a wrench: more expensive certainly, but a very nice touch if you feel the need to alter the ride height on a regular basis.

Of course, don't forget that you must fit shorter than stock dampers when radically lowering your Bug. They're readily available for use on the front and save the hassle of constantly bottoming out suspension.

Next on your shopping list will almost certainly be a set of wheels for your Looker. While you can make good use of your standard rims on a budget Bug, there's no denying that a set of custom mag wheels will do more to transform the appearance of your Bug than anything else, save a roof chop. Popular choices are EMPI-style eight-spoke wheels for four-bolt applications and EMPI-style five-spoke rims for older five-lug Bugs. However, popular as these rims are, they are not the be all and end all of Cal Look styling.

It could be that you want your Bug to look like it came straight off the drag strip, in which case there is probably no substitute for a set of Centerline wheels or other similar spun aluminum race-style rims. In Britain, Compomotive manufactures a whole range of split-rim

The ultimate wheel for a Cal Look Bug? Many people think that a polished Porsche 911 rim is the way to go. Early types came in 5½" or 6" widths.

right
To fit Porsche 911 wheels you will need to have the stock brake drums redrilled using a special jig like this. Use wheel studs, not bolts.

(three-piece) wheels in a variety of styles which should cater for every taste as far as owners of four-lug Bugs are concerned. An added advantage of the split-rim wheel is that by mixing and matching rims you can arrive at a virtually infinite range of offsets and widths to suit every application.

In years gone by, the choice of specialist wheels for VW use was probably even greater than it is today, with British companies like Speedwell marketing wheels for what was perceived to be a growing market. Wheels produced by this company showed up in the USA under the, surprise, surprise, EMPI brand name as EMPI-BRM magnesium rims. Much sought after today, these wheels are prone to damage and corrosion problems thanks to the high magnesium content of the castings. Other popular wheels were the EMPI SprintStars, steel sculptured wheels seen in Europe under the Lemmertz banner. Available in both four- and five-lug versions, SprintStars were even offered by dealers as options on some promotional vehicles.

The traditional EMPI-style eight-spoke and five-spoke wheels are just that – EMPI *style*. Now that the EMPI company has ceased business (although the name lives on as a product line), wheel production too has long since ceased. That hasn't stopped somebody from capitalizing on the demand for these desirable wheels by casting replicas. However, whereas the originals

were all two-piece bolt-together parts, the current replicas are simple one-piece castings.

Sizes? The most common size – and indeed if you choose to use EMPI-style wheels you will have no other choice! – is 5½ width by 15" diameter with an offset designed to allow the wheels to be used under stock fenders without spacers or added flares. Although it is possible to fit wider rims under the rear, space does get a little tight, especially if the Bug has been lowered radically. When using Centerline or other race-style wheels, it is not uncommon to use a thin 3½"-wide rim at the front.

Gaining in popularity all the while are Porsche 911 wheels – the classic 5-spoke mags used on early versions of the German supercar – early because only on older 911s can you find 5½"- and 6"-wide wheels. More modern Porsches have considerably wider rims than can be effectively used on a Cal Look Beetle. There are two problems with using Porsche wheels: the lug pattern is different to that of a Bug (Porsche choose to use a small PCD 5-lug design wheel) and the inset (the amount of rim inside the center line of the wheel) is far greater than that of a stock VW rim, meaning that unless spacers are used, the wheels can end up being tucked too far under the fenders with possible clearance problems.

To get round the problem of the differing lug fittings, it will be necessary either to fit wheel adaptors or to have

left
Many of the original Cal Look cars ran these EMPI-BRM wheels produced by the Speedwell company in Great Britain. They are much sought after today.

A nice example of a resto-Cal, so called because it tastefully combines the low stance of a Cal Looker with the originality of a restored Beetle.

your existing brake drums/discs redrilled and to have studs fitted in place of the usual VW bolts. In the latter case you will almost certainly need to use spacers between the wheels and hubs. As adaptors are usually fairly thick themselves, no spacers are necessary to achieve the desired offset.

Tire choice has become almost a personal thing today, whereas in the early days there was only one way to go: Michelin ZX in 135x15 size at the front, 165x15 on the rear.

Removal of the side chrome helps give a Cal Looker a slick appearance. Note the clever use of graphics and the quality of black paintwork.

Now it doesn't take too much to realize that a slim 135-section tire is going to be extremely stretched when fitted to a 5½"-wide rim. For everyday street use, it's better and safer to fit 145-section tires. The overall diameter is not much greater than that of the smaller tire, but the section is almost half an inch wider, requiring less of a stretch to fit.

At the rear these days you will frequently see 185/70x15 tires used which have the same rolling diameter as the 165-section tires, but a section almost one whole inch wider: altogether a better choice as far as road-holding is concerned, but then, since when has Cal Look had much to do with sportscar handling?

All these wheel and tire configurations will fit under stock fenders without problem and, allied to a good lowering job, will transform your Bug into a cool looking car even with no other modification. However, true Cal Looking goes further still.

Once upon a time the style was to have as much chrome as the eye could handle. Detroit went chrome-crazy in the fifties and many European manufacturers followed suit. Volkswagen, as conservative as ever, never allowed itself to be too carried away, but by the end of the fifties even the humble Bug had chrome trim down each side, along the running boards, and around the windows – all this in addition to the dazzling array of plating on headlight rims, bumpers and hubcaps. For Cal Look there's only one way to go – get rid of that chrome!

Removal of the side-trim will reveal a line of holes in the flanks of the car which will need to be filled prior to painting. The best way to do this is to use a MIG-welder

Another difficult but worthwihile modification is the removal of the door hinges and drip rail. This makes for a very clean and simple look.

California Look styling shown to good effect with Rossi headlamps, a total lack of chrome trim, neat frenched turn signals and Porsche wheels.

HAZ·719

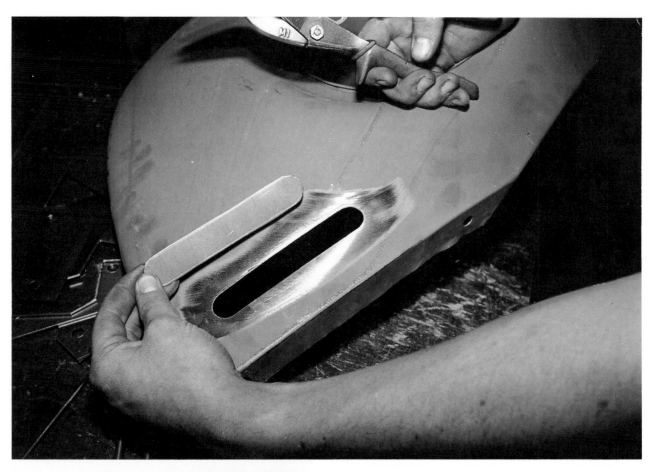

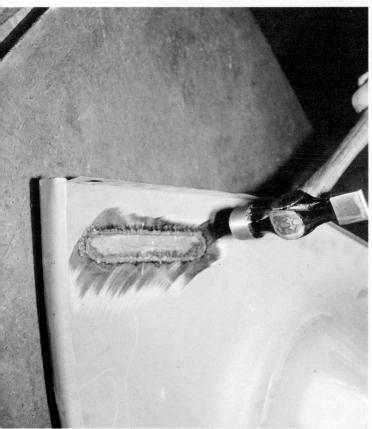

To do a perfect job, hammer the welds as you work. This will help reduce the amount of grinding and filling that will otherwise be necessary.

Late-model fenders have large bumper slots. You will have to cut a piece of sheet metal exactly to size and weld it into place using a MIG-welder.

which won't cause any distortion of the surrounding panel, but if one is not available, then a conventional gas welder can be used to fill the holes with braze. Take care when doing this, though, for the heat can cause distortion. The secret is to work a little at a time and keep wet rags nearby to cool the panel.

The same process can be used to fill the holes left by redundant trim down the centre of the trunk lid or where badges used to be. However, if you wish to remove the bumpers and horn grills, then you will need to make up a patch panel out of sheet metal to weld into position. Once welded in place, grind down the excess material, fill with a plastic filler and smooth off into the surrounding contours.

A commonplace modification to carry out is that of fitting early body panels to late-model Bugs. Although superficially the panels look interchangeable, in almost every instance some work will be involved to get things to fit. Take fenders for instance. Pre-'68 Bugs used sloping headlights which most people reckon look more cool than the later upright lights. The problem with swapping the parts over is that the valance (the panel between the fenders at the front of the car) changed slightly to accomodate the later shorter trunk lid. Although the early fenders will bolt onto the later Bugs, the alignment is not quite perfect. The only way to arrive at a perfect solution to the problem is to change all the front end sheet metal! This is an instance where you have to weigh up the expense and effort against the final appearance.

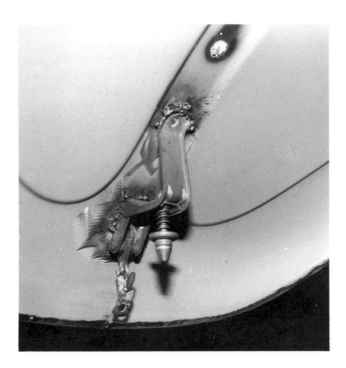

The stock Volkswagen headlamps are not the best in the world for looks or output. Replacing them with Cibié conversions helps a great deal.

left
To get rid of the unsightly stock hood **handle** it will be necessary to weld the lock mechanism to the underside of the trunk lid as shown here.

The rear of Alain Reuckens' Bug looks for all the world like that of a modified early model, but that rear window is a fake, as is the deck lid.

Removing the stock vent windows and replacing them with one-piece glass is another way to make your Bug look cleaner. Check the fit carefully.

The ultimate body modification is the roof chop. The amount of work involved is truly daunting as the roof needs to be cut into many pieces.

To end up with a good finish, no matter how expert you are, it will be necessary to use plenty of plastic filler. The result is simply stunning.

At the rear, as long as your Bug is a '67 or earlier model, then any type of deck lid will fit – as long as it comes from a pre-'68 Bug. So an old 'W' deck lid will bolt right on to your '66, no problem, the only hassle being that you'll need to modify the lock mechanism to suit. To convert a later 'square' rear end to the early style, you will need to change the rear panel to suit. Note that the '67 1500 Bugs had their own style of deck lid – it was almost as long as the earlier rounded type, but featured a squared-off end like the later short style fitted to Super Beetles and most '68-on Bugs.

Changing doors between years is no problem as long as you remain aware of the changes in window size over the years. Nothing looks worse than a pre-'65 Bug which has been equipped with a pair of late, large window doors. People have done such things, and worse, though heaven only knows why!

One trick you'll sometimes see is frenched indicators. Frenching – or tunnelling as it's sometimes known – is where the light unit is recessed into the surrounding body panel. If a round indicator unit is used, then a piece of steel tubing can be used as the housing for the light unit. At the back of the car, you can use the standard rearlight housings reversed and welded in place in holes cut into the fenders for a frenched 'stock' look. The lens units are simply bolted in place on what is effectively the reverse side of the original mounting.

Inside the Bug, the original Cal Look doctrine used to be to make the vehicle look as much like a Porsche as possible. European reclining seats with plaid inserts and matching door trim panels, rear seat, etc., were all part of the overall look. Add to this a full complement of VDO or Porsche gauges, a leather-bound steering wheel, trick gear shifter and possibly a rear roll-over bar and the result is a Cal Looker that looks fresh out of Stuttgart!

Today, styles have changed somewhat, with dashboards cut out and replaced with a smooth skin, allowing freedom to place gauges and hi-fi wherever you please. In vogue too are Plexiglass or polished aluminium dash inserts, the latter being perfect for would-be drag racers. Center consoles are very much part of the Look as the factory dashboard offers little in the way of accommodation for mega-watt stereo systems with their tape decks, equalizers and pre-amp units. However, it cannot be denied that, for the ultimate in style, skinning over the whole dash and leaving just one gauge – usually the speedometer for obvious reasons – is the way to go. Nothing beats the simplicity of such a dash, especially if the gauge has been repainted to match the rest of the car. Hide the switchgear away underneath the dash, add some graphics to compliment the exterior color and away you go.

Seating is obviously a personal thing, but there is little doubt that you cannot go wrong with a pair of Recaro seats from a Porsche. However, it could be that your budget doesn't stretch that far, so why not take a stroll down to the local wrecking yard and run a tape measure

top right
The stock dashboard can be a little limiting in appeal, so many people cut the original out and replace it with a sheet of polished aluminum.

bottom right
An aluminum dashboard allows you to fit whatever instruments you like, where you like. Those being fitted here are from the German VDO range.

over some seats; plenty of the modern Japanese cars have some pretty neat seats which would look the part in any self-respecting Bug. However, don't ignore the possibilities offered by standard Bug seats, especially those fitted to early models. If finances don't stretch as far as a set of expensive aftermarket seats then those stockers might just fit the bill. Any good upholstery shop will be able to recover your chosen seats in anything from original material to genuine leather. The only limit is the size of your wallet.

So what about body color? There was a time when you had to paint your Bug Porsche India Red or forget the whole thing! Perhaps not quite, but certainly India Red has been the mainstay of the Cal Look scene for many years. Today, however, anything goes. Wild graphics

Less is more! Simple treatment of dashboard on this Bug shows that you need not get carried away with gauges. Graphic detailing is stunning.

have taken the place of simple straight colors, with shocking pinks and candy greens replacing plain whites and stunning blacks.

When it comes to choosing paint for your Looker, it is worth spending a fair amount of time looking through magazines and at other people's cars to see what does and doesn't work. For example, you may like the idea of painting your Bug pink with lime green scallops, but aside from which shade of pink to choose, there is the matter of what shape those scallops should be. Only by

Early California Look Beetles featured single color paintwork, but today practically anything goes, as can be seen on this radically painted Bug.

looking at other people's cars, sketching out some ideas on a sheet of paper and refusing to rush into things will you end up with what you want. Spraying a car is an expensive, time-consuming business and it pays to get it right first time.

Sketching out ideas before starting up the compressor and blowing on some paint is easily the best way to find the perfect (for you) color scheme. Now it may be that you don't have sufficient skill to dash off a neat freehand drawing of your car, but don't worry. Looking through a copy of your favorite magazine, search out a large side-on photograph of a Bug. Trace off the outline with a fine pen and then photocopy the result onto a dozen sheets of paper. There you go – all you need now is a set of colored pencils or marker pens and a few hours of your time to

dream up all kinds of original paint schemes, one of which might just be the one you're looking for.

Just one final tip when conceiving your Cal Look prize-winner. The whole essence of California Look is simplicity, backed up with some horsepower if you so wish. Avoid over-fussy interiors, garish paintwork (definitely no Metalflake or murals, OK?) and overfat wheels!

Remember the old adage: less is more. It could have been made for the Cal Look.

HIGH 'N' STYLISH
High-flying Bajas, low-riding Roadsters

The Baja kit consists of a set of seven panels: four fenders, trunk lid, nose piece and rear panel.

While many people believe that the essence of customizing a VW is to take what Dr Porsche gave us and make the most of it by smoothing out the factory sheet metal, there are many others who feel that the stock Bug appearance leaves a lot to be desired. They might feel, for instance, that the Bug just doesn't look tough with a low-to-the-ground Cal Look stance, or isn't stylish enough with a tin lid for weather protection. For these people the Baja Bug and the Bug Roadster conversions are the way to go.

The first of these, the mighty Baja, is so called because it resembles those Bugs raced by many a hardy soul in the infamous Baja 1000 off-road race in Mexicali. With chopped-off fenders, raised suspension and toughened up running gear, the Baja Bug is ideal as an on- or off-road vehicle where more protection is required than can be offered by a 'glass-bodied Beach Buggy.

The Roadster on the other hand is for those who desire a Bug with all the attributes of a Porsche Speedster without the added complication of cost! Take one Bug, slice off the roof, trim down the windshield and add some new glassfibre panels for a unique and truly stylish roadster look.

Although seemingly at odds with one another in overall style, the concepts of both the Baja and the Roadster are very similar; both retain most of the stock sheet metal and all the running gear of a Bug. They drive like a Bug without suffering from the shakes and rattles that plague so many 'glass-bodied kitcars and buggies.

Let us take a look then at the creation of each of these machines, starting with the high-riding Baja Bug.

Basically a Baja conversion consists of a set of glassfibre body panels which are attached to a cut-down Bug bodyshell. The panel kit consists of two front fenders, two rears, a nose and trunk lid, and a rear finishing panel. The fenders are attached using the stock fender mounting bolts, while the nose and rear panel require attachment using blind rivets, sheet-metal screws and/or epoxy adhesive.

Baja kits are available to fit any type of Bug, although the most popular are those which may be used on torsion-bar front end Bugs. Fitting any one of the many Baja kits available on the market is much the same regardless of who manufactured the panels in the first place, so the guidelines illustrated here should apply in most instances.

When buying a Baja kit, check closely the quality of the panels, not only in terms of whether the gel-coat is cracked, or if the 'glass is thick enough, but also to see if the fenders are twisted, or whether the bolt flanges on the fenders are wide enough to accept 8mm bolts with large washers. Note the finish to the edges of the panels, whether the hinge mountings on the hood are strong enough to take the loads of a stock hinge and whether the panels are symmetrical, side for side. This last point may sound strange, but many Baja kits – and Buggies for that matter – have been designed 'by eye' with the result that all too often the panels just don't quite match up when the car is viewed from front on. It is not unknown for a pair of Baja fenders to vary in width by as much as a whole inch! Check before buying, rather than risk tears in the workshop a week before a show.

The process of fitting a Baja kit begins with removal of the stock bumpers and fenders. This is a good opportunity to check out the condition of the car in general, and to cure any rust that may be starting to take hold. Don't worry about the rear bumper mountings, or the spare wheel well – they'll soon be disappearing anyway as you cut the car to take the Baja kit. Fitting a Baja conversion can save you repair time too, see?

At the front end, you'll need to establish where to cut the stock sheet metal in readiness for the new nose. The best way to do this, assuming that the kit doesn't come with a set of instructions (they seldom do) is to take off the stock trunk lid and bolt up the new Baja part. This way you'll soon see just how short the Baja is compared to the stock Bug. Now with a marker pen, make a mark at the point where the new trunk lid starts to curve in away from the stock quarter panels. This will be the upper end

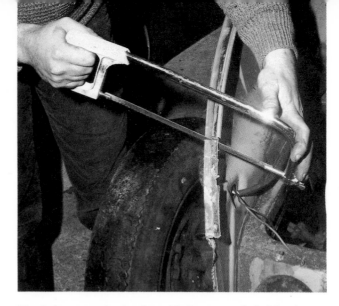

The Baja conversion begins with the removal of all fenders, trunk lid and deck lid. The first cut is the most daunting! Measure accurately.

of the cut you are going to have to make in a minute. Now take a look inside the spare wheel well, and drill a hole out through the bottom corner on each side, through the inner fender (quarter panel). This establishes the bottom of the cut.

Next, draw a line between these two points with the marker pen and then draw another line one inch forward of this first line. With your hacksaw, or air-chisel, cut down this second line and do the same on the other side of the car. Cut, too, across the bottom of the spare wheel well so that the front of the car is now hanging loose on the trunk release cable. Disconnect the cable and cut through the conduit it runs in before discarding the front valance and attached sheet metal.

Phew! Once you've got over the shock of cutting into your prize Bug, the reason for drawing the two lines with the marker pen had better be explained. The first line is the correct one, or near to it, but the second gives you an

With the front panels in place, already you can see the Bug taking shape. You don't have to remove the doors, but doing so helps access to the interior.

The Baja Bug got its name from the Baja peninsula, home of spectacular off-road racing. This Baja racer seems to take everything in its stride.

inch of sheet metal to play with in case you got your measurements wrong first time around! It's far easier to grind back excess metal with an angle grinder than it is to weld in new metal because you've trimmed away too much.

Offer up the new nose and you'll see that the trunk lid will follow nicely the contours of the panel. If it doesn't then you've either got a bad kit or a bent car. The chances are quite high either way, it seems. The only remedy here is to cut and shut the Baja nose panel until the trunk lid lines up perfectly. Once you're satisfied that the alignment is good, drill through both the nose piece and the quarter panel and fix the former with some pop-rivets.

Only when you are totally happy with the way things look should you break out the resin and hardener and begin to 'glass up the inside of the trunk where the new panel meets the old. Do the same on the outside too.

The front fenders will need to be offered up to the car and the mounting holes marked with the marker pen. Take care to ensure that the fenders exactly align with the nose and that the holes you drill for the mounting bolts are not too close to the edge of the 'glass. The chances are that the fenders will be a little twisted – 'glass panels' often are as the manufacturers are all too keen to get the panel out of the mold in order to start laying up a new one! Result? A panel that distorts as the resin cures.

Use large diameter washers when bolting up the fenders – these will spread the load a bit and help prevent the fender from cracking when you tighten the mountings. The same holds true at the rear when you come to start that.

Talking of which, now remove the rear bumper and fenders if you haven't already done so, and the engine

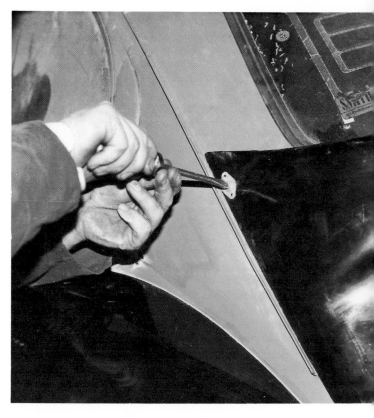

On their example, UVA chose to fit the rear panel with Dzus fasteners for easier access to the engine and the oil cooler which was to be fitted later.

At the rear you can see the way in which the quarter panels have been trimmed back in readiness for the shorter fenders. Tires look good.

too if you wish. It sure does help access. Unbolt the engine lid and don't forget to disconnect the wire to the license plate light. The upper end of the cut you're going to make is easy to establish: all you have to do is offer up the new rear fenders and see where they finish at the back edge. This will be on the panel round the edge of the engine bay, just below the louvers on each side and adjacent to the end of the rain gutter or drip rail. The bottom end is found by drilling out through the front corners of the engine bay where the firewall, side panels and closing panels (the ones on each side of the engine bay to the side of the spark plugs) all meet. The drill hole will come out somewhere just behind the body mount on the quarter panel.

Again, break out the hacksaw and grinder and cut down the line drawn between the two points – you'll need a chisel to persuade the panel to come off thanks to some metalwork round the engine bay. Once this is removed you've got yourself half way there.

Now offer up the rear finishing panel – the one which fits across under the rear window of the Baja. You will probably have to trim it slightly so that it sits comfortably between the drip rails, but apart from that it's a straightforward panel to fit, needing only some sheet metal screws, Pop-rivets or Dzus fasteners to locate it. If you so wish you could use some plastic filler to blend the panel into the surrounding roof for a professional look, but be warned, you may end up with cracks showing if you decide to use your car off-road, thanks to flexing of the body panels.

Fitting the rear fenders follows the same pattern as the front. Just take your time and your patience will be rewarded with a neat, factory look. It is up to you whether you fit the fender beading or blend the panels in with plastic filler. If you're sure that you are never going to run the Baja off road, then maybe you can get away with blending in, but the most sensible approach would be to buy some new fender bead and use it. After all, you can never be too certain that you won't have to remove or replace a fender at some time in the future.

On most Baja kits you will need to remove the headlamp buckets from your old stock fenders and then 'glass them into the new ones, having trimmed a hole large enough for them to fit. Most Baja fenders will accept late-type (post-'67) VW headlamp units. At the back, offer up the stock tail lights and draw round them with a marker pen to allow you to mark where to drill for the mounting bolts. Always double check that the lights will sit symmetrically on both fenders – nothing looks worse than a Baja with lopsided tail lights! Don't forget too that you will have to earth all electrical components such as turn signals that are mounted onto 'glass panels.

Once your Baja kit is fitted you have some good old-fashioned basic bodywork to do in readiness for paint. Incidentally, while on that subject, don't forget that the 'glass panels will need a coat of special etching primer before regular priming – the etching primer is a mild acid which eats into the surface of the gel-coat ensuring that the primer and top coats don't flake off. Do not forget to do this.

Aside from the abbreviated bodywork, the most significant aspect of any street Baja conversion has to be work on the suspension system to give that high-riding, off-road stance. Now, strange though it may seem, the work required (unless you are going for a full-house competition conversion) is much the same as that needed to produce a low-riding Cal Looker! No, you don't start dropping the front end on the ground, or turning the rear trailing arms on their splines to get the tail in the dirt, but you can still fit Sway-A-Way adjusters on the torsion beam to raise the front up from stock. All you need do is mount the adjusters in a higher position on the torsion tubes.

At the back you can remove the trailing arms and move them round by a spline, but remember, you are effectively lengthening the distance between the upper and lower damper mountings. This means you are going to have to think about fitting longer than stock shocks at back and front.

An alternative method of raising the car can be to fit coil-assisted shocks (sometimes called coil-overs because they feature a coil spring over the top of a simple shock absorber unit). These are readily available in over-stock lengths, and many also feature adjustable spring mountings just like on a motorcycle shock so that you can fine tune the ride height. These units are inexpensive and help to beef up the suspension for mild off-road use.

If you want to take the competition look a stage further, you can fit twin shocks at the rear – race vehicles use multiple dampers because single units could not cope with the rigors of racing on rough terrain. Bolt-on multiple shock brackets are available for Bugs and they locate on the three bolts that hold the trailing arm to the axle at the rear. You will have to fabricate some top mountings and have them welded to the frame, but that isn't a problem.

The correct choice of wheels and tires is a vital part of establishing the Baja look – no way can skinny stock rims with radials convince your friends that you are about to ride the dunes of Pismo Beach! Although for sand use thin front wheels and tires are recommended, for the full Baja race-ready look you'll need to go for some wider rims and fat off-road tires such as Goodrich All-Terrains mounted on white eight-spoke wheels. Sizes? A six-inch rim at the front backed up by a pair of eights at the back should give you something to start with. Fatter than that and you start to learn all about horsepower loss through excess drag!

A word of warning about using fat and, especially, tall tires on your Bug. The standard gearing in the transmission is designed for freeway use, with a high fourth gear and final drive. Fourth is almost an overdrive and allows the engine to laze along at lowish revs to save wear and tear and fuel. By fitting large diameter rear tires you effectively raise the overall gearing by a very noticeable amount. The result is that the car feels sluggish, especially when getting on the move, and you may find yourself changing down into third far more often out on the road as even the slightest hill can be too much for the poor Bug.

You can avoid these problems by fitting the lowest overall final drive available – commonly the 4.375:1 as used in 1200 and 1300 Bugs – or by using aftermarket gear ratios. The latter route is by far the best as you can tailor the ratios to exactly suit your driving needs, but of course, like all good things, you have to pay for them! Aftermarket gear ratios are not cheap.

It is also worth noting that fitting larger tires to the front makes the speedometer under-read (i.e. give the impression that you are travelling slower than you really are). This can be rectified by having the gauge

The Baja conversion is both practical yet eye-catching and tough. The exposed and chromed engine will take some keeping clean on the beach.

Engine access couldn't be better on a Baja Bug – note stinger
exhaust system. Even a street Baja like this can see some
limited off-roading.

recalibrated by a specialist, the alternative being to have a good explanation for the police officer when he pulls you to the side for driving ten miles an hour over the speed limit!

To complete the Baja style externally, you will need to fit front and rear bumper cages – you will almost certainly be legally required to fit some sort of protection round the engine to prevent pedestrians from burning themselves on the exposed exhaust system. Cages are readily available from most VW specialists and bolt up to the front torsion bar tubes and to the rear shock and transmission mounts. Not only do they give your pride and joy some much-needed protection, but they also serve as excellent places to mount driving lights and CB antennae.

Other external fittings which add to the look are side protection bars which bolt on in place of the stock running boards. These normally bolt to the stock mounts on the rocker panels and an extra one drilled through the rear quarter panel just behind the door. They help to protect the lower part of the body when using the vehicle off-road, and give valuable protection to the somewhat fragile 'glass fenders when driving in everyday traffic.

Because the engine is fully exposed on a Baja Bug, it is vital that at the very least you clean up the stock unit and keep it that way. Add some simple chrome goodies and paint detailing and already it starts to look brighter. You have to replace the stock muffler system, fitting an off-road style unit in its place. These are available in a variety of styles, the most common being an upswept header system with either a single or a dual 'quiet'

Every Baja ought to run front and rear bumper cages – the front one being an ideal location for additional driving lamps such as these Cibiés.

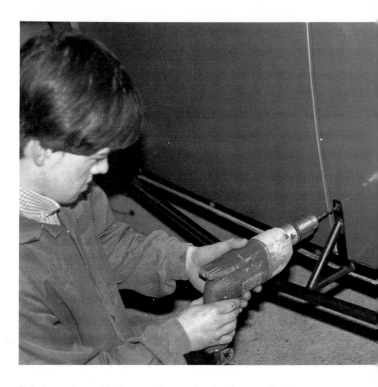

Side bars give added protection to the fenders and help safeguard occupants in the event of a T-bone accident. They replace running boards.

muffler arrangement. Popular too are the 'dual cannon' type which, despite looking particularly aggressive, are not as efficient as a good dual muffler and are twice as loud.

Even mild off-roading will require fitting some kind of protection to the underside of the engine in the form of a sump shield, and probably pushrod guards too. Pay attention to transmission mountings – beefed up, heavy-duty mounts are readily available and save on broken transmissions when your Bug is used off-road. You will also need to ensure that the carburetter receives a supply of clean, well-filtered air at all times. Use off-road

Russell Fielding's street Baja is simple yet very nicely detailed. It goes to prove that you don't need to get carried away to look stylish.

air filters on the carb(s), tucked well away to prevent accidental damage. The same goes for any extra oil fittings you may choose to fit: keep them well away from exposed areas.

If your laws allow it, then fit roof-mounted long-range driving lamps such as KC Daylighters – they really help to give that competition appeal. At the very least, fit a pair of high-power driving lamps to the front nudge bar,

above
Rear of this Baja could benefit from an engine cage, not only to protect that exhaust system but also to prevent pedestrians touching the hot header.

below
Interior of a Baja should be functional, but that does not mean to say it cannot look professional. Note the aluminum door panels and dash.

The Roadster conversion – this is from Wizard Roadsters in Britain – looks its most appealing from the rear. This is a very stylish example.

To build a Roadster you will need one Beetle, a set of panels, basic handtools, gas welder and plenty of spare time. It's worth the effort.

as the stock VW lamps need all the help they can get. For protection against stone damage, it is a wise move to fit covers to the lights when not in use, and stone-guards to the headlamps.

Turning to the interior of the Baja, the most common approach is a semi-race look with bucket seats, roll-cage and a series of accessory gauges. Add some full-harness safety belts, a fire-extinguisher (a worth-while addition to any car, regardless of style) and your Baja will soon look ready to take on the worst that Mexicali has to offer.

The great thing about street Bajas is that they look oh-so tough and yet are extremely practical everyday vehicles. They have a stock heating system, they have roll-up windows, they have a rear seat – in fact they would seem just like a stocker to drive if it wasn't for those tires and the high-riding stance. If bad weather is a problem for you, then the Baja might be the answer to your prayers.

The Roadster, on the other hand, is for those who enjoy driving in the sunshine, hood down, wind in the hair. Like the Baja, the Roadster is still a practical everyday vehicle, especially as it is now possible to buy removable hardtops. This way you get the best of both worlds.

Essentially, the Roadster kit consists of a new rear deck panel, engine cover, windshield surround, hood and all the fittings necessary to complete the conversion, including the vital strengthening bars that fit under the rocker panels. You can go a stage further and replace the stock fenders with wider ones so as to accept aftermarket rims and rubber, or replace the trunk lid with the smooth, no-molding type available from the Roadster kit manufacturers. The kits shown on these pages came from Wizard Roadsters in Britain and are available to fit all but the curved-screen Super Beetles.

The conversion begins with stripping the donor car of all trim, inside and out, along with window glass – it is not a difficult job to reduce a Beetle to a sorry-looking shell, but you will need the assistance of a friend to take out the glass if you don't want to risk breaking it. The interior trim can be largely retained for refitting later, although most owners will want to fit aftermarket seats and some form of custom upholstery to give a professional look to the car.

Before cutting strength out of the Bug, it is wise to begin by adding some, welding on the strengthening bars that run along the underside of the car by the rocker panels. These are designed to follow the contours of the floorpan and give the body some much-needed rigidity once the roof is removed. You are now ready to start surgery.

The front windshield pillars are cut at a point given in the instruction manual that comes with the kit, and the 'B' pillars are cut also. At the rear, a gently curving cut is made from the rear edge of the side windows down to a point determined once more by measurement, but roughly in line with the top of the engine firewall. As this is a double-skinned area of the car, you will need to measure and accurately mark both inside and outside before cutting. This done, you can go ahead and cut the roof away before lifting it off (mind those sharp edges left by the hacksaw!). You are now at the point of no return!

top right
Additional bracing has to be welded across rear of Bug to make up for loss of roof. Similarly, bracing bars are welded along edge of chassis.

bottom right
Epoxy glue is used to bond new deck panel to existing sheet metal. Use sheet metal screws or Pop-rivets to hold in place until completely dry.

The top edges of the rear quarter panels need to be cut every few inches to allow the inner and outer skins to be bent in towards each other. They should ideally be welded together for a neat, strong finish. The next stage is to trial-fit the rear deck panel and check that there are no rough edges of bodywork that will need to be ground down.

Once you are happy with the fit, you will need to weld in the strengthening brace that runs from one side of the car to the other. This is absolutely necessary if there is to be any structural integrity in the 'new' car. With this done, fit the new firewall supplied with the kit – this is 'glassed into place.

You are now ready to fit the rear deck panel finally. With the panel offered into position, use epoxy resin to 'glue' the new panel to the old, and some sheet metal screws to temporarily hold things in place would be a good idea until the epoxy sets. The new firewall will

Roadster conversion starts with the removal of entire roof assembly – there is no turning back once you have reached this point! Take care.

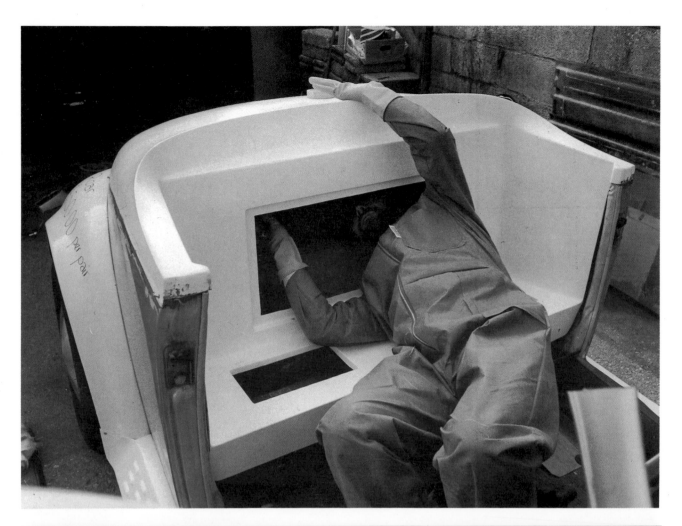

Cutting the windshield surround down to size – followed by the doors. Rear edge of doors will need some work to ensure lines follow through.

need to be sealed to the deck panel with 'glass mat, and access to this area is available through a cutout in the 'glass panel behind where the rear seat would be.

The deck panel can be blended into the original quarter panels with plastic filler, taking care to do a good job as this will be the area most examined by friends and rivals when you're finished! If you are running an unvented engine cover, you will have to cut a pair of cooling holes in the side of the engine bay to allow the fan to draw air in from under the rear fenders. This is easily accomplished using a jig-saw or saber-saw.

The doors are next for surgery, with the front pillars being cut to line up with the abbreviated windshield surround. At the rear edge, the pillars are cut off flush with the tops of the doors and new closing panels fitted to tidy things up. A new windshield surround is supplied with the kit and this is now ready to be offered up and fixed securely in place.

It is worth noting that the new windshield glass is flat,

top left
Glassing up the rear deck is not a pleasant task! Access to underside is limited. Bond in new firewall at the same time – and wear hat and gloves.

bottom left
This is what your Bug should look like once the new deck panel has been blended into the stock sheet metal. A good finish in this area is critical.

whereas the stock glass – despite appearances to the contrary – is slightly curved. Because of this, it is necessary to dress back with a hammer the lower sealing lip (where the sealing rubber normally sits) until it is straight, allowing the flat glass to be fitted.

To fit the engine lid, re-use the stock hinges, and expect to have to make a few trial fittings to get the alignment correct. A little patience here will, again, not go unrewarded. Access to the engine is somewhat restricted using a Roadster kit, but no worse than that of a VW camper.

Aside from 'minor' considerations such as respraying the car, fitting the hood, etc., the conversion is complete. The standard of finish of the components in these kits is very high and it is worth spending a little longer than you first intended when carrying out the conversion so that you end up with a Roadster you are truly proud of. It would be very depressing to have to spend the next few months or years making excuses as to why the back of the car isn't finished all that well. Be patient!

Should you wish to go a stage further, the manufacturers of the Roadster kit can supply new wide fenders, a smooth trunk lid, deep side skirts to replace the stock running boards, and a whole host of extras to make the final conversion appear as professional as possible. If the idea of a more weatherproof Roadster appeals to you, then it will be worth considering buying a removable hardtop. These clip or bolt into place and tend to follow the contours of the normal folding hood. They do much for the warmth of the occupants during a cold winter! The choice, as they say, is yours, but remember, there are many fine Roadsters on the road, and yours could be one of them.

above
Because new windshield glass is flat and original is slightly curved, you must straighten the lower sealing flange with a hammer like this.

below
Once you are happy with the trimming, the new windshield surround can be bonded into place. This will give the new glass much-needed rigidity.

above
If a windshield isn't supplied with your kit, you will have to make up a template out of plywood or heavy artboard. Have new glass cut.

below
If exposure to the elements doesn't appeal to you all the year round, then why not obtain a removable hardtop like this? It adds practicality.

Add a splash of color, some neat graphics, and you too can be ready to shoot the breeze in your very own roadster.

BUGGYING ABOUT
On the street and over the dunes

Is this what started it all? Original Kubelwagen (literally translated, Bucket Car!) was derived from Beetle and had impressive off-road ability.

When the Beetle was first seen upon this earth, it was the German military who took perhaps the most interest. Early testing showed that the little People's Car was not only an excellent autobahn cruiser, but possessed a ruggedness not seen before in such a vehicle.

It was not long, then, before work began on designing an off-roading road version for military use – the Third Reich's answer to the ubiquitous Jeep. The end result was the Kubelwagen (literally 'Bucket Car') which, despite its crude appearance, was a rugged machine capable of excellent cross-country performance even though possessing only two-wheel drive.

Many years later in Southern California (where else?), off-roading developed as a recreational pursuit thanks to the thousands of square miles of desert within a relatively short distance of some of the larger conurbations. Early recreational off-road vehicles tended to be very crude. Those that first saw the light of day as VW Beetles frequently ended up as bare floorpans with two seats and a home-made roll-over bar cresting the dunes at Pismo or Glamis. Effective? Certainly. Fun? Definitely. But stylish? No way.

The person who saw the need for a stylish yet simple and lightweight body to fit on to the VW floorpan was Bruce Meyers. With the advent of the Meyers Tow'd and Manx buggies the face of VW recreational off-roading changed dramatically. Many companies jumped on the bandwagon in the early 1960s on both sides of the Atlantic. Everybody went Buggy mad!

Meyers' concept was a simple one: to improve handling and responsiveness he shortened the floorpan by a little over a foot and then equipped it with a neat glassfibre body that resembled nothing that had ever gone before. By fitting the new vehicle – soon to be termed a Dune or Beach Buggy – with larger than stock wheels and tires, a roll-over bar and little else, it was possible to have fun on a weekend without having to spend a fortune. Building a Buggy was simplicity itself, only the chassis-shortening requiring any special skills, although soon enough there were any number of shops willing to take on such work. All you needed to get started was a Bug, some basic tools, a few buddies and a little spare time.

Since their earliest days, Buggies have been raced on both sides of the Atlantic. This photo from the '60s shows how little safety mattered!

Over the years, numerous styles of Buggy developed, some requiring shortened floorpans like the original versions, others designed to fit the stock floorpan. Hardtops, vans, pickups – they were all available as Buggy bodystyles, some very attractive, others plain ugly. All followed the same basic principles.

The starting point for any 'glass-bodied Buggy is a torsion-bar front suspension Bug – definitely no MacPherson strut Super Beetles here. The body will need to be removed and this is an operation that can easily be carried out at home in the driveway. All you need is the assistance of a few friends to help you lift the body clear of the floorpan. The procedure is as follows.

First thing to do is disconnect the battery and then go ahead and strip out the interior of the Bug. You could take out the glass too as this will save weight when you come to lift-off time. Remove the doors for the same reason. Next remove the fuel tank, taking care to block off the fuel line so as to prevent spillage,. With the tank removed it will be possible to undo the steering coupling and free the steering column. Note the horn wire – that'll need disconnecting too.

While you are under the trunk lid, you might as well remove the two bolts that hold the body to the top of the torsion bar assembly and then disconnect the brake fluid reservoir.

At the rear, take a look under the fenders and undo the two bolts (one each side) that secure the rear body mounts. If you can't see them at first, it's probably because they are covered in dirt and grime. Wire brush all the dirt away and then take a look near the top shock absorber mounting. See it now? Good.

In the engine bay, disconnect the electrics from the coil, carb and generator/alternator, and then, underneath the car, disconnect the wiring from the starter motor and solenoid, and the fuel line where it exits from the frame horns alongside the transmission. Do not forget to plug the fuel line.

From inside the car remove the row of bolts that secure the body to the floorpan under the rear seat area. Watch out for a couple of bolts which hide away right at the outer edges – they're often covered over with old soundproofing material and are easily overlooked. Underneath the car there is a row of bolts along the edge

left
The earliest Buggies were little more than stripped Beetle floorpans with crude roll-over bars. They soon made way for something with style.

above
One of the earliest and prettiest American-built Buggies was the EMPI Imp. Note that this example has a set of EMPI SprintStar wheels to match.

of the floorpan on each side and then two more on each side under the front heater channels. The latter are frequently rusted in place and can either break or tear the captive nuts out of the body. Don't worry as you won't be needing the body any more if you are building a Buggy.

At this stage you should be ready to lift the body off the 'pan. Well, in theory you should be, but experience shows that you almost always forget to undo at least one bolt somewhere!

Generally it will take about six of you to lift a body clear of the floorpan. A labor-saving way of doing things is to lift one end at a time and prop it up on some heavy planks supported by trestles. This way you can lift the body up from the 'pan and then wheel the chassis out from underneath. Using this method the author has carried out a body swop with the help of just one friend. It can be done!

With the body out of the way, it is an easy matter to remove the engine and transmission, along with the front suspension. Why should you need to do this? Well, you are never going to get a better opportunity to clean the floorpan and paint it, repair it and generally detail it ready for the shows. If you are building a short-wheelbase Buggy then you are about ready to take it along to a specialist shop for them to carry out the surgery.

The process of shortening a VW floorpan is not one we would recommend the average enthusiast to do for it is very important that the final alignment is absolutely perfect and that the welding is of the very highest quality. Also, you must get the amount of shortening just right, for obvious reasons! The actual operation is quite complex as you have to reduce the length not only of the floorpan itself but also of the gear linkage, fuel pipes, handbrake and heater cable tubes and the clutch and throttle cable conduits, all of which are found inside the backbone of the chassis.

You will need to have a new shorter rear brake pipe made up and have the gear linkage cut'n'shut to the right length. The conduits can be trimmed to length. As for the cables, well, you can either get new ones made up by a specialist or use a shortening kit available from one of the VW shops which allows you to reduce the length of the stock cables. Although the shortening kits are quite adequate, they can lead to cables parting company after a while, so perhaps the extra expense of getting some custom-made cables done to length isn't such a bad thing.

With the chassis shortening completed, the body can be mounted. Using a new body sealing gasket round the edge of the 'pan, the body can be lowered into position, taking care to ensure that it sits centrally both fore and aft, and side for side. You will almost certainly have to drill holes through from underneath (using the mounting holes in the floorpan as a guide) ready for the bolts you'll be using to secure the body, although some kits will come pre-drilled.

Once you are happy, use some new nuts and bolts with large washers to bolt the body up finally. The stock, shaped, washers should be used under the edge of the floorpan, while the new large washers will be used inside the car to spread the load against the 'glass and help prevent cracking.

Few if any Buggy kits are so complete that they don't require a fair amount of head-scratching on the part of

Buggy construction begins with the removal of the old Beetle body. This is not difficult as long as you have the assistance of a few good friends!

the builder when it comes to jobs like routing the steering column and mounting the fuel tank. More often than not there are no detailed instructions and so the builder has to work out the exact location of mounting holes, etc., himself. The rule here is to think logically (often difficult at three o'clock in the morning when you've sworn that you wouldn't go to bed until the body was finished!), measure carefully and check, check and re-check.

Most kits have a body that is in two parts, the nose of the Buggy being a separate panel incorporating the windshield surround. Others have a separate aluminum frame around the glass, but the mounting of the nose follows the same principles. You will need to trim the panel carefully so that it sits comfortably on the main molding, ready to be secured using bolts or sheet metal screws. As a finishing touch, use some fender beading as a sealing strip along the edge of the nose panel.

If your Buggy has a windshield surround integral with the rest of the molding, then you will almost certainly have to trim the aperture to make the glass fit correctly. Be careful not to trim too much away or you run the risk of having the windshield blow in on you at speed on the freeway. However, trim the molding insufficiently and you can end up cracking the glass as you try to fit it into an aperture that's too small to allow for the rubber seal around the edge.

The dashboard molding usually comes without provision for any gauges, so you will have to establish the best positioning of them to suit your driving position. To do this, bolt in the seat you intend to use and, using cardboard circles as dummy instruments, tape the

'gauges' into position on the dash and check for the best place as far as you, the driver, are concerned. If you are wondering what gauges you should fit, then apart from the obligatory speedometer you should consider a tachometer, oil pressure and temperature gauges, maybe a voltmeter and, simplest of all, a clock. You'll be amazed at how useful you'll find the latter and yet many people neglect fitting one when they've got the opportunity to design their perfect dashboard layout.

top
Now you can see why the Bug lends itself to Buggy building. Floorpan is usually shortened just behind handbrake assembly by approximately 14 inches.

above
The dashboard of this Buggy shows considerable thought on the part of the owner — note how all switches are grouped together over on the left.

Choose switchgear carefully – many accessory switches are poorly made and break easily. What you are after is a set of switches that not only look 'factory' but function so. In fact, why not take a look round the local wrecking yard and check out the switchgear available on some of the modern imports?

Choosing seats for a Buggy is important – no way can you use the stock VW seats in a vehicle like this! Popular styles are competition type 'bucket' seats or hi-tech recliners. It all depends on what kind of image you are trying to put across with your Buggy. If you really do intend to use it regularly off-road then it makes a lot of sense to go for an easily cleaned vinyl finish to the seats, with rubber mats on the floor as the finishing touch. However, the vast majority of Buggies never see any dirt and can benefit from interior trim that wouldn't look out of place in a Porsche.

No matter what style you are after, you must run a rollcage of some kind in an open Buggy, even if it is nothing more than a single roll-over bar with a pair of bracing bars to the rear. It is absolutely vital that you fit bracing bars to a single hoop like this as otherwise, in a roll-over situation, the main hoop will simply fold back and offer no protection at all. Such insurance is cheap. Better still would be to run a full cage with front hoop and bracing bars joining the two, as well as rear braces going down to the frame. Door bars – or what would pass as door bars if the Buggy had doors – would also be a good bet so as to offer some side protection in the event of someone T- boning you. Safety first? You bet!

Similarly, pay particular attention to the mounting of seat belts in a Buggy as the upper stock mounting will have disappeared now that the original bodyshell has been discarded. It is not enough to drill a hole through the roll bar and simply bolt the harness to it; you must make proper provision for bracing the mounting. Many Buggy owners run full-harness race-style belts and perhaps these are altogether the best solution given that it is all too easy to be thrown out of a Buggy in a relatively minor accident.

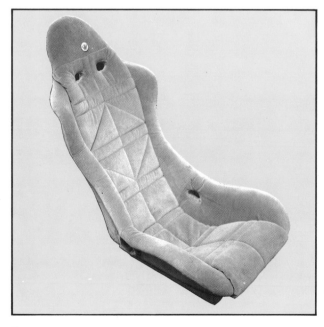

If you plan to go off-road with your Buggy then seats which offer good support will be necessary. This style has provision for full harness.

When creating a Buggy, there is the question of what style to follow. Do you want to drive a pseudo-off-road racer, or would something along the lines of a low-riding Super-Street Buggy be more to your taste? The typical Buggy of days gone by had a Metalflake body, huge chrome rims and fat street tires. Today they are somewhat more varied in their appearance, with high'n'mighty off-roaders rubbing shoulders with monster-engined, ground-hugging street racer Buggies. Somewhere in between there lies the more commonplace custom Buggy with its graphic paintwork, polished mag wheels and chromed engine. They might share the same bodyshell, but that's about as far as the connection appears to go.

The traditional 'glass-bodied Buggy tends to see little serious off-road use, its place being taken by more specialized tube-chassis vehicles such as the Chenowth. Stronger, lighter and better handling, the tube-framed vehicles run rings round their VW-floorpanned brethren when it comes to off-road action. However, that is not to say that the traditional Buggy has no place off-road – far from it. With a little thought, the humble shortened Veedub can still provide hours of fun for its owner.

above
GP LDV (Light Delivery Vehicle) was an interesting departure from normal Buggy styling. Produced by GP Vehicles in Britain, it was very practical.

left
A traditional Beach Buggy in Metalflake finish. This is by far the most popular style with its fat wheels, simple roll-over bar — and surfboard!

left
Rails such as this British example are the logical progression from the glassfiber-bodied Buggy. They are lighter, stronger and better handling.

below left
In the USA, highly developed rails such as this Chenowth single-seater rule the short course events. Note the multiple rear shocks.

If the off-road look is for you, then think seriously about running a full roll cage as described earlier. Competition-style seats, full-harness belts, an extinguisher and a host of gauges will all help the image. Externally, you'll need to use white eight-spoke wheels or hi-tech race wheels such as Centerlines if you want to project the Baja-ready image. Tires will need to be of the all-terrain variety, with the rears tall and fat (don't forget the price to be paid in increased overall gearing though).

For paint, a striking single primary color such as a rich yellow or brilliant orange would look good, especially when backed up with some race-style signwriting or plenty of 'sponsor' decals.

For the complete off-road look, add some KC Daylighter driving lamps and a nerf bar at the front. Fat wheels and tires add to the impressive look.

White eight-spoke wheels are available from a variety of sources and are an inexpensive addition to any Buggy. Tires shown are ideal for road use.

To continue the competition theme, mounting a pair of KC Daylighter driving lamps on the roll cage and a whip aerial on the rear end will help matters along, but you will need to pay attention to protecting the underside of the engine and transmission, just like on the Baja Bugs described in an earlier chapter. A full-length skid-plate running under the engine and trans will be an absolute necessity, as will healthy front and rear bumper cages. The latter will of course keep you legal, too, in places where the law is not keen on exposed engines.

The choice of exhaust system runs pretty much parallel with Baja thinking, although more Buggies seem to run the 'dual cannon' type. Perhaps it's because Buggy owners are more extrovert than other VW owners!

If the street racer approach is your choice, remember that you'll have to have plenty of horsepower to back up the image. It's no use your Buggy looking like it can run 9-second quarter miles when in reality it can barely make it the whole way down the strip. You will need to give serious consideration to running costs and insurance though, if this is the route you want to take. A nitrous-oxide injected, turbocharged 2-litre motor in a street Buggy might sound like fun, but in the wrong hands it could be a lethal package.

Instead of running the Buggy high off the ground, using a pair of Sway-A-Way adjusters in the front beam will allow you to get the nose in the dirt, and turning the trailing arms on the torsion bars at the rear will get the back down, so already the whole image of the traditional Buggy is being turned on its head. Hi-tech split-rim racing wheels (Compomotive, Gotti, etc.), with skinny Michelins on the front and low-profiles on the rear will all help the street-race look. Wheelie bars would be a styling 'must' in this instance – in fact with a super-hot motor in a lightweight 'glass Buggy you'll probably need them!

Whatever style you go for, the fact that everything mechanical is on display in a Buggy means that you must pay a lot of attention to detailing those parts that are normally hidden from view on a sedan. The engine is the prime area (just like on Baja Bugs) and needs plenty of detailing if the car is to look good. Volkswagen engines are not the world's most oil-tight units, but that shouldn't stop you from keeping yours clean. Once you have rebuilt the engine, or at the very least had it steam-cleaned, you will have little difficulty in ensuring that it stays looking good. All it takes is a few minutes each weekend to wipe over the tinwear and whatever else may have got dirty during the week.

There are so many chrome dress-up items available these days for the air-cooled Volkswagen engine that there is no excuse for not adding a bit of sparkle to the old flat four. Have the cooling tin sandblasted or chemically stripped and repainted in a color to match or contrast with the body. Wire separators help keep the ignition leads tidy, while simple goodies like transparent distributor caps, finned valve covers and chrome oil caps can add that final touch. There is also such a range of billet-look aluminum parts on offer from any number of companies that it is relatively simple – if not necessarily cheap – to give your engine a very hi-tech look without having to go anywhere near a milling machine or lathe.

The ultimate Buggy? Wild 'Manxed Out' show car is a popular exhibit at VW shows in SoCal. The stock floorpan has been replaced by a tube chassis.

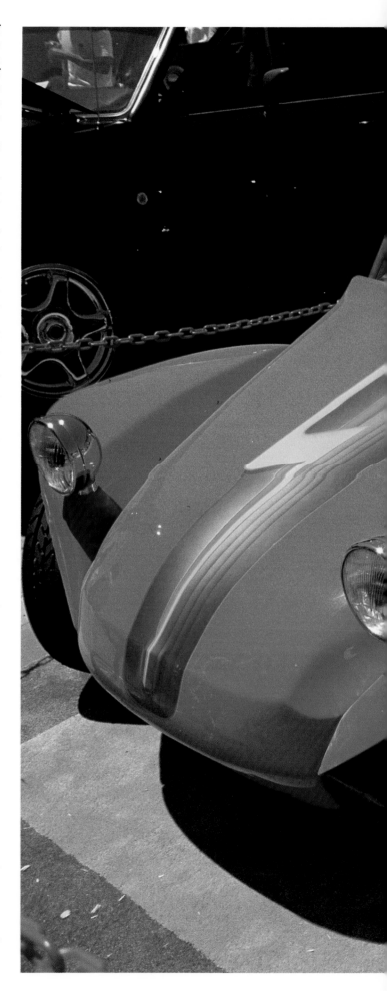

Ah well, you can't win every time! The driver of this rail has just learnt the hard way about how strong his VW front suspension really is!

The question of exposure of components brings to mind the other matter: exposure to the elements. Buggies are far from being the most comfortable vehicles in the world, especially where rain and cold weather are concerned. Buggy heating systems usually leave much to be desired in standard form as there are no heater channels like on the Beetle to duct warm air through to the feet. All you normally get are heater vents behind the seats which do a great job of keeping the back of your seat warm and little else. If you still want to run a Buggy in a cold climate, use heater trunking to duct warm air through from the back. It can be hidden under carpeting and can be positioned to allow warm air to exit under the front of your seat. Anything is better than freezing in a cold winter.

The fold-down hoods supplied with many Buggies (or available as an extra) do little to keep out the elements when things get bad. You should really consider one of these as a 'get me home' aid rather than a fully weatherproof set-up. Some Buggies are available with removable or even fixed hard-tops – the perfect answer if you prefer to be warm and dry at all times. But if that's the way you feel perhaps a Baja Bug is the thing for you. At least you get to keep all the good things about a Beetle while still enjoying the off-roadability of a Buggy.

Without a doubt, Buggies are some of the most fun machines on four wheels. They are relatively inexpensive to build, can be driven on a daily basis and yet have a style all of their own. If you feel the need to go a stage further, a tube-framed car could be the way to go. Offering all the benefits – and more – of a traditional Buggy, the custom-chassis 'rail' has the added advantages mentioned earlier of greater strength, lighter weight and better handling. It is relatively easy to construct and is available in a whole host of styles, from four-seater, rear- engined 'family' models to wild single-seater, mid-engined sand racers. Most popular are the traditional – if such a word can be used in this context! – two-seat, rear-engined rails. More fun than they have a right to be, these rails may not exactly be the ideal way to get to work each day, but they sure help blow the cobwebs out at weekends!

The engine of any Buggy is open not only to the elements but also to close inspection. Why not make use of the many dress-up goodies on offer?

Radical super-street Buggy with cut-down windshield and
ultra-low stance looks all action even sitting in the parking lot
at a California VW show.

PEOPLE'S CAR POWER!
Getting the most from your flat-four

When you consider that the last thing in anybody's mind when the Beetle was conceived was making it turn 10-second quarter miles, it is amazing that today there are so many Bugs capable of quite astronomical performance. The first Bugs were designed to be autobahn cruisers capable of transporting two adults and three children from A to B at a speed of 100kph (62mph) with an average mileage of 33mpg. Bearing in mind the severe cost restraints placed on the project in terms of the final selling price of the People's Car, it is a wonder that anything of any interest to the sporting enthusiast resulted from the exercise.

However, history has shown that right from the very earliest days of VW production people couldn't resist tinkering with the Bug, not the least of these being Dr Porsche himself, who soon realized the potential by building 'specials' that resulted in the first of the Porsche marque.

In the late 1950s there was a not inconsiderable array of tuning components available for the old '30-horse' engines, ranging from superchargers by Judson through to the superb Okrasa gear. It is likely that but for the efforts of Okrasa in Germany VW tuning might not have developed as it did, or the factory even develop the engine as it did. Okrasa, better known today as Oettinger, which currently manufactures a large range of tuning components for the water-cooled range of VWs, listed a vast selection of equipment ranging from stroker crankshafts to dual-port heads (in a day when every head from the factory had tiny siamesed inlets) and twin carburetor set-ups. The equipment was way ahead of its time then, and even today, given the same basic engine and materials, it is hard to think that anyone could come up with anything better.

The Okrasa kit, consisting of a pair of their dual-port heads (not to be confused with the factory-produced dual-port heads that were to appear ten years later!), special manifolds and dual Solex 32mm PBI carbs from a Porsche 356, resulted in a massive 33% increase in peak power. Now with hindsight it is easy to say that 33% of not much is still not a great deal, but in those days a fully Okrasa-equipped Bug was almost as quick from zero to sixty miles per hour as an MGA or 1600 Porsche 356. In today's terms, think of a Bug capable of taking on a Porsche 911 away from the lights. And yes, it is possible, as we hope to prove.

Starting at the beginning, let's briefly consider the usefulness of the stock VW engine with regard to tuning. Common sense tells us that it is perhaps best to ignore the old 30-horse engines (used up to 1960) as there really

is no available tuning gear around today – unless you happen to stumble on some NOS (new old stock) Okrasa gear. Even the humble 1200 engine used throughout the sixties and indeed up to the present day is not really a prime candidate for performance modification (but don't despair 1200 owners – there's some hope for you around the corner). No, the best engines to modify have to be the models produced from August '69 onwards as they feature a greatly improved oiling system and are available in 1300 and 1600 capacities with a longer stroke crankshaft which had superior oilways to the earlier '1300/1500' crank.

The 1200 engine (strictly speaking 1192cc) features a 64mm stroke crank and 77mm bore cylinders. It is a good reliable engine in stock form and delivers the goods exactly as the factory intended. The main problem from the tuning point of view is that early models had no camshaft bearings – the cam ran direct in the crankcase – meaning that it is impossible to repair worn journals short of having a machine shop line bore the camshaft gallery to allow you to fit cam bearings. In addition, the crankcase is not as heavily braced as the larger engine's, meaning that it is not really suitable for high-performance applications. The cylinder heads are of the single port variety – i.e. they feature siamesed inlet ports as opposed to the more efficient twin inlet ports of the later 1300 and 1600 engines – and the ports themselves are very small, being designed to restrict the 'revability' of the engine. Although it is possible to do some parts swopping between the 1200 and 1600 units, it is hardly worth the effort.

You still want to tune the 1200? OK, follow the course taken by the author many years ago when funds were somewhat restricted. Have the flywheel lightened to about 13lbs, open out and smoothe the inlet and exhaust ports, match all the manifolds to the ports correctly, balance the bottom end assembly and smooth off the rough edges of the combustion chambers. Machine the heads to give about 8:1 compression ratio and then replace the stock carb with a dual-choke progressive Weber 28/36DCD carb on a manifold adaptor. Even with the stock exhaust system this brought about a massive reduction in zero to sixty time, bringing it down from an original 27 seconds to about 14! Tame by today's standards, but fun in its day.

Right, back to reality and what you can do to the engine sat out back in your Bug. Before going any further, check to see exactly what model engine you have. The following guide to engine number prefixes should help.

D	1200 from August 1965
F	1300 from August 1965 to July 1970
H	1500 from August 1966 to July 1970
AB	1300 from August 1970 to July 1973
AR	1300 from August 1973 to July 1975
AD	1600 from August 1970 to July 1973
AS	1600 from August 1973 to January 1980

The above prefixes relate to the European market.

The following are for 'Export' models:

B	1600 from August 1968 to July 1970 (USA only)
E	1300 from August 1967 to July 1970
L	1500 from August 1967 to July 1970
AC	1300 from August 1970 to July 1972
AE	1600 from August 1970 to July 1971 (USA only)
AF	1600 from August 1970 to December 1977
AH	1600 from August 1971 to January 1976 (USA only)
AJ	1600 from August 1974 to December 1977 (USA and Japan only)*
AK	1600 from August 1972 to July 1973 (USA only)

* **This is the L-Jetronic fuel-injected engine**

For performance purposes, any engine with a two-letter prefix starting with the letter 'A' is a suitable base for tuning. The crankcases are stronger, they have better oiling systems and are plentiful. However, once you have identified the 'base' engine, there are several checks to run through before embarking on that journey into the unknown.

Volkswagen engines tend to suffer as a result of high mileage and high revs, with the suffering manifesting itself in the form of worn main bearing saddles. This causes a drop in oil pressure and that is no good thing for an engine that relies so heavily on its oil, not only for lubrication but also for cooling. With the engine stripped down to a bare crankcase (and thoroughly degreased) take a good look at the condition of the main bearing saddles. If there is a ridge worn on them corresponding to the oilway on the back of the bearing shells, then the case definitely needs line boring. This is a machining process that opens the bearing saddles out to an oversize on the outer diameter of the main bearing shell. It could be that a crankcase is no use at all, being worn beyond acceptable limits. Currently bearings are available in up to 1mm oversize – if you have to remove more metal then that to take care of the damage than the case is scrap. Likewise, if when you bolt the two halves of the crankcase together you can see daylight between the mating surfaces, then again the case is only fit for the scrapheap. You will simply never get good oil pressure again with such a case.

Look for cracks behind the flywheel, a consequence of poor machining for large-bore cylinders or high heat build up due to poor cooling, prolonged high revs, etc. Although

This is the first place to check a crankcase for wear. If the main bearing saddles show signs of pounding then expect to line-bore the case.

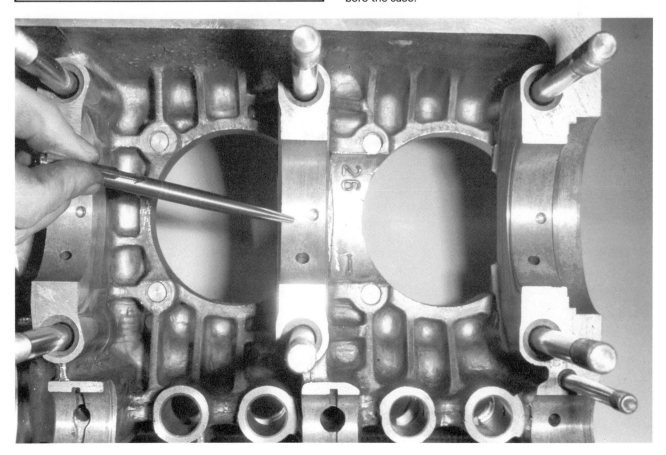

Turning your everyday Beetle into a tire-smoking street racer is not out of the question. This road-legal Super Bug runs low 12s on the strip.

such damage can be repaired, it is probably not worth the effort. It goes without saying that you should reject a crankcase that has suffered damage through being dropped or involved in a rear end accident. There are plenty more fish in the sea.

If you are going to retain the standard crankshaft – and it is perfectly acceptable to do so for many road applications – then measure up the diameter of the main and rod bearing journals. If they are outside the limits set by the factory then you will have to have the crank reground by an experienced machine shop. Hold the crank by one end and tap it on the webs with a hammer – it should ring true. If it doesn't then suspect a crack somewhere. You can always take the crank along to a machine shop and have them crack test it for you if there's any doubt in your mind.

Again, if you are planning on using the standard con rods, take them along to your machine shop and have them checked for straightness. You would be surprised how

Where it all began – the complete Okrasa conversion as fitted to Roy Worsley's '51 split-window Bug. The power is increased by 33% over stock.

many rods have been bent over the years!

Take a look at the flywheel, and more importantly its friction surface. If there are signs of scoring then reckon on having the face reground to rid the flywheel of such damage. Look also at the surface where it bolts onto the crankshaft: are the dowel holes OK?

Once you have made sure that your basic engine is sound you need to decide early on whether your finances allow you to go for a warmed up engine of stock capacity or for a bored and stroked full-on powerhouse. We'll start with the basic tuning for road use and work our way through some of the alternatives available to the VW enthusiast.

The most basic bolt-on tuning component has to be a tuned-length exhaust system. Fitting requires nothing more than removal of the stock muffler and bolting up of the new tubular headers. Mufflers for these are available in a variety of styles, the most popular being the single or dual

Later crankcases use threaded inserts to locate cylinder head studs. Check to see if they have pulled. Early cases can be fitted with these inserts.

Crankcases that have had a hard life suffer from cracks behind the flywheel in this region. Many builders weld in a strengthener to add support here.

'quiet' types. As the name suggests, this type of muffler is not as loud as others, but its free-flowing design makes for good horsepower. Don't expect your Bug to become a Porsche-eater with just a set of headers, but it will feel and sound a whole lot better.

Next in line for replacement is the stock carburetor. The factory fitted small-bore Solex carbs which are just about adequate to allow the Bug to stagger up to its top speed and hold it there, but are not much use when you start making real performance demands on the engine. There is a whole variety of after-market carbs available for the Bug, ranging from the old Holley Bugsprays to the modern single and dual Weber or Dellorto systems. Many people will tell you different stories about what is and is not right for your car, but if you still have the stock capacity – say 1600cc – then you cannot go far wrong with a single Weber progressive twin-choke carb. Progressive? That means that one choke (throat) opens before the other, allowing you to drive around on one half (in effect a small single carb) and then crack open the other choke when you need the extra power just by putting your foot on the floor.

Progressive carbs are a great idea for those people concerned about fuel economy and yet still wanting to do a little stop-light racing on a Friday night! Most such carbs will require a special manifold to allow fitment to a stock VW engine. The original manifold is simply too restrictive for anything much other than the stock carb. Fortunately, VW made it easy for us on their dual-port 1300 and 1600 engines – the center section of the manifold is separate

from the two ends, being equipped with rubber hosing to mate up and make an airtight seal. This helps reduce the cost of an aftermarket system as only the center section of the manifold needs replacing to make way for the new carb.

If the engine capacity has been increased from stock, or you have gone ahead and carried out other mods such as porting and polishing the heads, changing the camshaft, increasing the compression, etc., then you could fit a single 40mm dual-choke carb such as a Weber 40IDF or Dellorto 40DRLA on a suitable manifold. Although these carbs can work on a stock 1600 engine, they really are a little large and can result in some pretty bad mileage figures.

Now one consequence of fitting an aftermarket carburetor of almost any sort is that the distributor advance will be up the creek. This is because the factory saw fit to rely on inlet manifold vacuum to operate the advance mechanism of the distributor. Change the carb and manifold and the vacuum changes. The answer is to fit an all-centrifugal distributor such as the traditional Bosch 009 type or the more modern 050 model. Either of these will restore your car's performance, but do not expect a Bosch 009 to improve the performance of an otherwise standard engine: it won't, despite what your friends may say.

Now is a timely (sorry about the pun) point to mention ignition timing on your Bug. The VW flat four engine is very particular about ignition timing, or more to the point, about over-advancing of it. Do not ever run more than a maximum of 32° total advance on your Bug. This works out to approximately 10° static advance, but don't rely on static timing for accuracy. Always check with a timing light (strobe). You have been warned!

So, without even really getting dirty you have a new exhaust system, a new carburetor and a new distributor all residing under the engine lid. Out on the road, assuming the rest of the engine is in good order, you should feel a very healthy difference in the performance of the car. No longer will you have to sit behind overloaded trucks – just drop down a gear and drive on past. It will be like driving a new car.

Assuming that you still don't feel up to the task of dropping out the engine and splitting the two halves of the crankcase apart, all that remains open to you is to fit some high-lift rocker arms. The standard rockers have a ratio of

Check the stock crankshaft journals for wear with a micrometer. Look in your manual to see if it is within tolerances. Regrinding can save crank.

bottom left
The first stage in tuning will probably be to replace the stock muffler with header set-up. Quiet and glasspack mufflers are shown with stinger.

Exhaust systems come in all shapes and sizes. The dual quiet system at top is intended for off-road Baja/Buggy. Note 'Rallye' system on left.

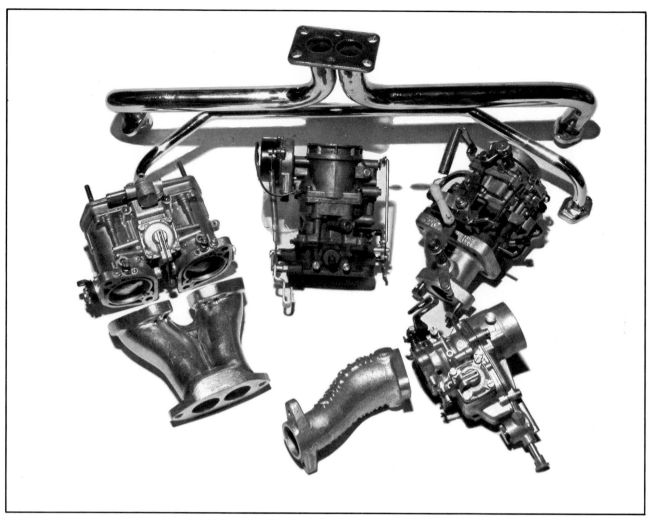

above
When it comes to carburetors, the choice is vast. Weber 40IDF on left, Holley Bugspray (centre with manifold), Nikki and Weber 34ICT on right.

below
A simple installation featuring dual Solex-Kadron carburetors and plenty of chrome dress-up goodies. An engine like this need not cost too much.

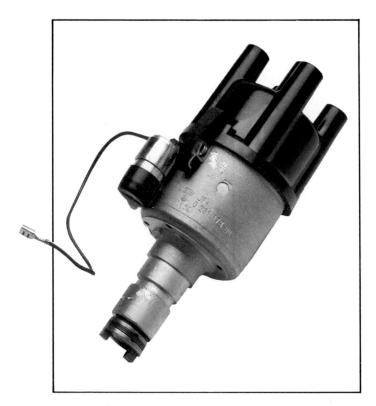

Fitting a Bosch 009 all-centrifugal distributor will help an engine with aftermarket carburetor system to run with a correct ignition advance curve.

1.1:1 (ie 1mm of lift at the camshaft lobe becomes 1.1mm of lift at the valve) on 1300, 1500 and 1600 engines. The poor 1200 got stuck with 1:1 rockers. Down at your local Volkswagen performance shop you'll find high-ratio rockers available in 1.25:1, 1.4:1 and 1.5:1 ratios, all of which can be used to successfully boost the performance of your engine by increasing the lift at the valves. Although the duration of the camshaft is not affected (well, strictly speaking it is slightly, but not to any great extent), the engine will produce more usable power. Usable because it is an increase in valve lift that is largely responsible for a boost in torque and bottom end power. This is what you want for everyday driving – your new carb and muffler will help the top end performance. Valve duration, the length of time a valve remains open measured in terms of degrees of engine rotation, is what affects top end power. This is why all-out race cams have high advertised durations.

Well, that's what you can do with the engine still in place. Remember, it's no use at all trying to hot up an engine that is worn or at all suspect. If the engine has covered more than about 30,000 or 40,000 miles think hard about tuning it without taking a look inside. If you have no real idea of the history of the car, then definitely take a look inside. Tuning is a great way of showing up weaknesses in an engine.

OK, so out with the jack and drop the engine on to the workshop floor, for this is where things start to get a little more serious. It could be that you simply want to carry out some cylinder head mods, in which case you need do no more than remove all the cooling tin and unbolt the heads. Check the valve guides for wear by waggling the valves (once the springs have been removed!) from side to side. If there is a lot of side play then the guides, usually the exhaust valve guides, will need to be replaced. At the same time – and indeed it is worth doing whether the guides are worn or not – you should replace the exhaust

valves as they are the weakest link in the VW head. Too many engines over the years have been destroyed by a dropped exhaust valve head.

If you poke your finger down the exhaust port you will immediately become aware of the sharp bend that the escaping gases have to negotiate on their way to the headers. This is the first thing to remove on a VW head, and it can be smoothed out into a gentle radius with the aid of a grinding tool run off an electric drill or an air-compressor. Finish off with some fine abrasive paper. Check the exhaust gaskets against the header flange and then against the port on the head. Ensure that the header, port and gasket all align correctly, and use the grinder to overcome any inaccuracies.

The same goes for the inlet port, although on dual-port heads it isn't as bad as the exhaust port. You will usually find that just under the valve seat the port is not very smooth. Again blend this into the surrounding area and gently enlarge the port in general. Once more check the alignment of the manifold, gasket and port and correct where necessary.

Check your stock heads for cracks between the spark plug and the exhaust valve seat. This can be costly to repair and may not be worth the effort.

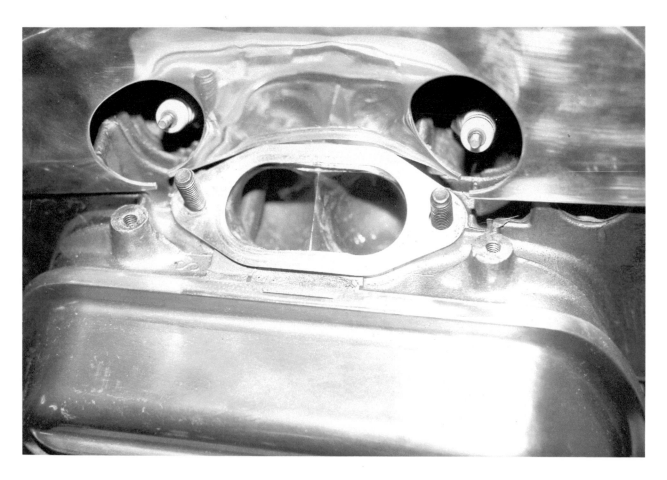

Radically reworked stock head displays much attention having been paid to the inlet port.

Simple work like this can make a big difference to the VW engine and the way it breathes. Taking things a stage further and machining the cylinder head for increased compression is a job for the machine shop. The combustion chamber needs to be flycut for greater depth, which has the effect of reducing the volume of the space between the head and the piston. It is vital to check after machining of this nature that the volume of all the combustion chambers is the same, otherwise the compression ratio will vary from cylinder to cylinder.

Do not exceed a compression ratio of 8.5:1 on a daily-driver engine. Today's poor fuel will only result in detonation if you do, and detonation is the kiss of death to a VW engine.

When you have the heads machined for a higher compression ratio (CR) you will either have to space the rocker assembly away from the head by a similar amount, or use shortened pushrods. This is because any flycutting of the head will effectively move the rocker gear closer to the camshaft, thus upsetting the angle of the rocker arms. This will lead to premature wear of the valve stem tips and the rocker arms themselves.

The most obvious step to take next is to increase the capacity of your engine by fitting a big-bore piston and cylinder kit. Some can be fitted without machining the crankcase – for example it is possible to uprate your 1300 to 1600 with only machining of the cylinder head being required. You can carry out this conversion using a set of used factory cylinders. You could also go for 87mm

cylinders, which will fit a 1600 crankcase without machining and result in a capacity of 1641cc. This is quite a worthwhile conversion and relatively inexpensive due to the lack of machining costs. Again, a 1300 will need those heads opening out to take the larger cylinder bore.

Perhaps the most commonly used conversion is the 88mm (1679cc with stock crankshaft) big-bore kit. Although it is possible to buy such a conversion with specially machined cylinders that allow you to fit them to a 1600 without opening out the heads, we would recommend you pass it by in favor of the thicker type that require flycutting of the cylinder heads. This way you get a better sealing surface between the cylinder and the head, and thicker cylinder walls into the bargain.

Going any larger than this will require machining of the crankcase where the cylinder slips into place. A 90.5mm bore cylinder kit will result in a capacity of 1776cc, while a 92mm kit will give you 1835cc, both using the stock 69mm stroke crankshaft. Either of these conversions is good, with the 1776cc kit being especially recommended for road use as the cylinder walls are that bit thicker where it matters.

A brief word about pistons. You will see advertised big-bore cylinder kits with either cast or forged pistons. Although the cast are slightly less expensive, we would recommend you go for the stronger forged type.

Next up for change will be the camshaft. Do not make the fatal mistake of choosing a camshaft that is too radical for a) your engine and b) your driving needs. A small displacement VW engine simply cannot handle too much camshaft duration or lift. It will make the engine less tractable and give very poor consumption. Similarly, if your driving consists of heavy stop-start traffic on the way to work every day, the last thing you want is an engine that coughs and splutters until it gets to 4000rpm thanks to a full-race camshaft being fitted. If you really like the idea of bragging about what cam your car runs, then buy the one that suits your driving but tell your friends you've got a secret new cam inside the crankcase that allows you to drive everywhere at 1500rpm yet comes on like gangbusters at 5000rpm. They might even believe you.

This may sound rather whimsical, but do not underestimate the damage a badly chosen camshaft can do to the drivability of your car. Always err on the side of caution and go for one of the tried and true grinds like an Engle 110 or 120. These cams didn't earn a sound reputation by making cars undrivable.

If you are changing the camshaft in your engine for one of the hotter street cams like an Engle 110, then it is worth thinking about having the valve size increased in the stock heads. By far the most popular choice is a set of 40mm inlet valves and 35.5mm exhaust valves. You could buy a pair of heads across the counter or have your own modified by a VW speed shop. Either way you will make a vast improvement to the engine's breathing capabilities.

Today there are several companies advertising their own big-valve heads for VWs, with names like '041' (actually a VW factory head produced in South America with larger than normal valves), 'Eliminator', 'Hi-Flo', etc. Never before have there been so many heads to chose from. Eliminator heads have become very popular, being billet castings as opposed to reworked VW heads. They feature larger and straighter inlet and exhaust ports and more meat around the combustion chambers to allow for deeper flycutting. They are excellent value for money and have been used with success by the author on his street-strip VW without problem.

As we say, for road use, bearing in mind that fuel quality is falling every year, have the heads machined for a compression ratio of around 8.5:1.

When changing the valve size, swopping the camshaft and doing anything else that will allow and encourage you to use higher revs than stock, you must change the valve springs. Uprated single springs are available as are dual and even triple set-ups. The latter are primarily for competition use, although a hot street motor will benefit from having duals fitted. These require machining of the

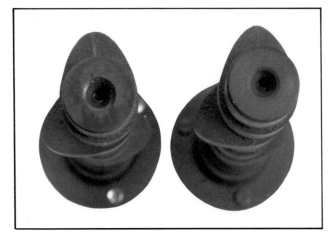

Although not at first obvious, these cams are very different. One on left has much longer duration than the other. Note fatter cam lobe.

valve guide boss to fit – another job for the machine shop.

To go with these high-rev springs you need to think about swopping over to heavy-duty valve retainers and collets. The former are available in chrome-moly, aluminum and even titanium, although these are only intended for racing use due to their high cost. Heavy duty pushrods should also be fitted at this stage, of which more later.

So at the moment we have ourselves the making of a pretty useful engine. A capacity of 1776cc, Engle 110 camshaft, Bosch 009 distributor, 40mm x 35.5mm valves, 8.5:1 compression ration, Eliminator heads and the start of a hole in the bank balance! What's next?

To make the most of this combination, you will need to look for a pair of carbs and manifolds. The best system to go for would be either dual 40IDF Webers or dual 40DRLA Dellortos on cast manifolds with a crossbar throttle linkage. These are tried and tested carburetors which are

The difference between older single-port cylinder heads and twin-port type is plain for all to see. Twin-port heads are the only way to go.

guaranteed to give you good performance with few hassles. If dual carbs are beyond your budget, then a single 40 or 44IDF Weber or 40 or 45DRLA Dellorto on a suitable manifold would be worth considering. At least you could upgrade to duals at a later date. Stay away from dual 48IDA Webers on the street – these are race-only carbs that may look really cool but do nothing at all for consumption or drivability.

Are we there yet? No way! There are some vital aspects that we've been saving to last, not because they're of secondary importance, but because talk of them won't inspire you to build a hot VW motor in the same way that reading of dual Webers or high-lift camshafts will. We're talking lubrication and balance here. Starting with the oil system, any mods to the VW engine will tax the stock lubrication set-up. At the very least you will need to fit an upgraded oil pump such as a Melling. Make sure you get the correct one for your car – later engines had a different style of stock camshaft (four rivets held the cam gear on instead of the earlier three) and the oil pumps are not interchangeable – the pump being driven off the end of the camshaft. If you are swopping the camshaft then the chances are you will be getting a three-bolt cam anyway, but if you stay with the stocker then do ensure you buy the correct pump.

To boost the oil pressure to the main bearings you can use an uprated oil pressure relief valve kit, which consists of stronger springs and deeper pistons than standard. You can even fit an adjustable relief valve kit for fine tuning of the oil pressure.

These two changes will help maintain adequate oil pressure under almost every circumstance, but will do nothing for the cooling. The VW engine relies a lot on the oil to help cool the component parts, so the lubricant has its work cut out. To ease the load it is vital to upgrade the stock

top right
The component parts of 1776cc engine for the road – note dual Dellorto carbs, counterweighted crankshaft, hot camshaft, uprated oiling system.

bottom right
Super-Flo 'heads are radically different to stock parts. The ports are larger and straighter than normal, requiring special inlet manifolds.

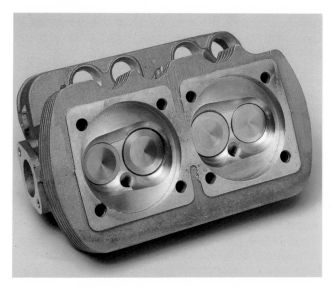

Street Eliminator heads are a popular conversion as they are very cost effective. To rework the stock head to this level would cost you plenty.

Weber IDF carburetor fitted to road engine – note use of good quality air filter. This will keep engine clean yet still allow it to breathe.

A single 44IDF Weber carburetor kit consists of carb, manifold, linkage, fuel line and all fittings. This is a good conversion on larger engines.

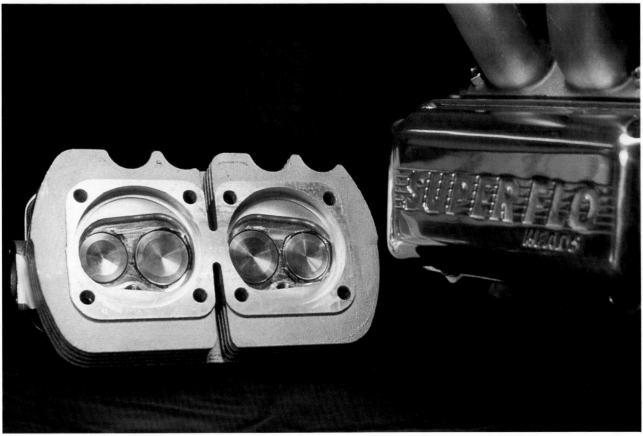

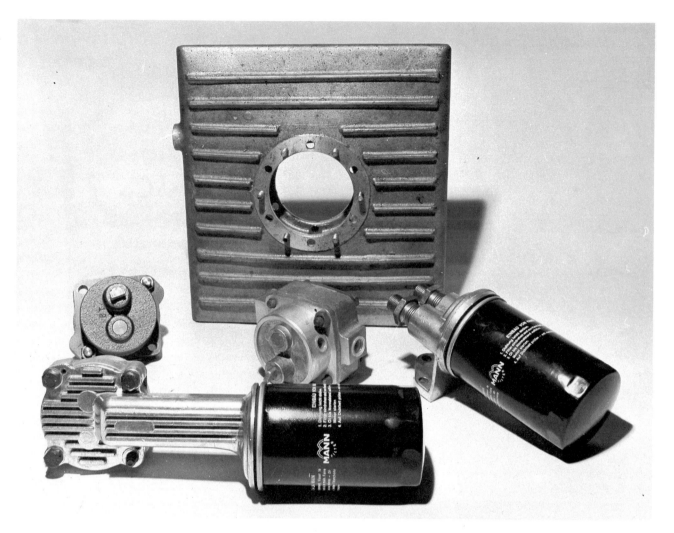

Uprating the stock oil pump is a must for long life. Deep sump at back will increase oil capacity. Filters are vital if the engine is to live.

oiling system by the addition of an additional cooler and filter. The latter is a most important addition as the standard filter system in the sump consists of nothing more than a crude wire mesh screen through which it is possible to pass rather large pieces of debris. Not much good for prolonged engine life!

You will need to have the crankcase drilled and tapped so that hose fittings can be screwed into the main oil gallery to allow for the exit and return of the oil. You can use an oil pump with an outlet on the cover plate and simply drill and tap the crankcase in one place for the return, but it is generally considered more efficient in terms of oil flow to drill the case in two places and use a stock pump cover plate. When you drill and tap into the lower main oil gallery to gain access to the oil, it is important to have the machine shop block off the gallery further down so that oil is forced to pass out of the crankcase and through the new oil lines, otherwise the lubricant will take the shortest route and simply bypass your new cooler or filter.

Run the oil out from the case and through a remote oil filter and then on to a cooler via a thermostat. The thermostat – or oilstat as it is often termed – will prevent oil from passing through the cooler until it has reached a predetermined temperature (usually about 75°C). At this temperature, a valve will open inside the oilstat and allow oil through to be cooled by the radiator. The return oil line from the cooler and thermostat will take lubricant back to the crankcase for circulation round the engine.

The question of where to fit an oil cooler on a Bug is a vexed one. It is important that the cooler should be mounted in a flow of cooling air, yet not be vulnerable to damage. By far the most efficient place to mount the radiator is under the rear window, where a maximum amount of air is channeled when driving along the road. However, this is not a very aesthetically pleasing location, and many opt for mounting the cooler at the front of the car under the bumper. This is great but for one thing: the length of oil pipe required for such an installation is truly massive, resulting in pressure loss along its length and problems of where to route the lines. The cooler could also be damaged in even a minor traffic accident, with catastrophic results to the engine if left running.

A favorite place to mount the cooler these days is either directly above the transmission or under one or other of the rear fenders, protected naturally by a stoneguard. Both of these locations have the advantage of being out of harm's way as well as being close to the engine so that only relatively short oil lines need to be used.

A final pair of additions to the oil system are a windage tray and a deep sump. The windage tray is a drilled metal baffle that fits in the stock sump and prevents oil surge. This is vital when racing and tackling the bends on the road. A deep sump is a bolt-on extension to the stock oil sump, doubling or tripling the capacity which, bearing in mind that the VW engine holds very little oil in the first place, is a

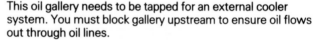
This oil gallery needs to be tapped for an external cooler system. You must block gallery upstream to ensure oil flows out through oil lines.

Lightening the flywheel, as seen on the right, will improve the response of your VW engine. This is a simple and inexpensive machine shop operation.

good thing to do. Watch out for gound clearance, though, on a radically lowered Cal Looker!

To ensure the maximum life from your engine and to make it more relaxing to use, it is vital to have the bottom end assembly balanced. This is a machine shop operation and not one that can be handled at home, other than to check for the relative weight of pistons. Using a simple beam balance, it is possible to establish which is the lightest of the set but to get them all to the same weight will still require the skills of a trustworthy machine shop. In general terms, the vast majority of piston sets sold will be of more than adequate accuracy in balance terms.

The kinds of operations you will be looking for your machine shop to carry out will be dynamically balancing the combined crankshaft, flywheel and clutch assembly, checking the balance, end for end, of the con-rods, piston matching, checking rods for straightness and perhaps lightening the flywheel, as a reduction in weight here will improve the response of the engine. At the same time, have them drill the crank and flywheel for eight dowels. This will help the flywheel stay on when the going gets tough. All this will do nothing for the visual appeal of your engine, but will do wonders for the feel and longevity of it.

The next stage of tuning will involve changing the stock crankshaft for a stroker crank – that's a special crankshaft with a longer piston throw than a stocker. All 1300/1500/ 1600 VW engines come from the factory with a 69mm crank – that means that each piston moves up and down the bore a total of 69mm during each revolution of the engine. Increasing the amount of piston travel by increasing the crankshaft throw will in turn increase the capacity of your engine. Long stroke cranks are available with a variety of throws, 74mm, 78mm, 82mm and 84mm being the most readily available, the first three being easily the most common. The main problem associated with using a stroker crankshaft in a VW engine is the matter of space

above right
For increased output, there is no substitute for using dual twin-barrel carburetors such as this Dellorto 45DRLA system. Ideal for 2-liters plus.

above
This stroker crankshaft kit uses restroked VW crank and modified Rabbit/Golf rods. The Gene Berg crankshaft damper is designed to reduce flexing.

within the crankcase – the stock case was designed for a 69mm crank and that's all. All the strengthening webs cast into the case are designed to clear the stock crank, rods, etc., but tend to get in the way when larger stroke cranks are used. What is needed is to clearance the inside of the crankcase by judicious use of a grinding tool. Particular attention must be paid to the area around the base of the cylinders where the conrods sweep close to the bottom of the cylinder bore.

To establish how much metal needs to be removed it is necessary to lay the crank and rods in one half of the crankcase at a time and gently rotate the crank holding each rod as if it were connected to a piston. Note that the rod bolts will get close to, and probably foul, the case near the cylinder. You must remove as little metal as possible, but still sufficient to allow a minimum of 0.040in clearance between the rod and the case. Check and double check. Take a look too at the clearance between the crankshaft and the camshaft – on some long stroke applications the crank balancing webs can actually touch the cam lobe. If this is not checked and remedied by careful machining of

COMPUTE
Displacement Chart

STROKE	Bore 83	85.5
64	1385	1470
69	1493	1585
74	1602	1699
78	1688	1791
82	1775	1883
84	1818	1929
86	1861	1975
88	1905	2021

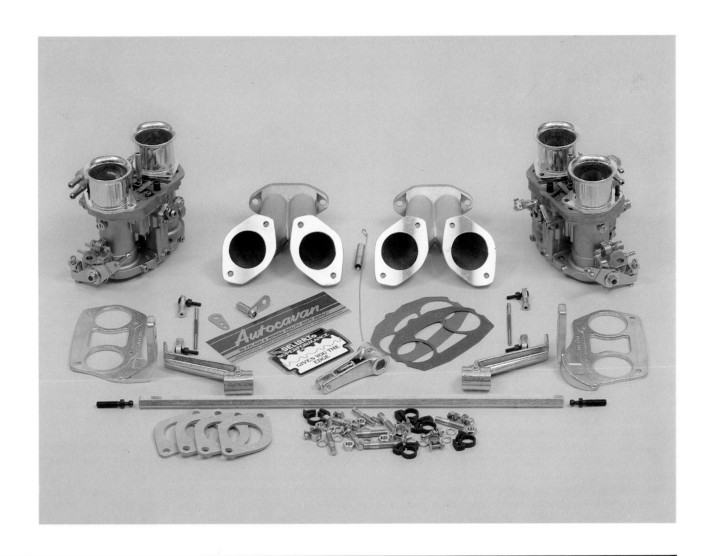

ENGINE DISPLACEMENT
For 4 Cylinder Engines in CC

87	88	90	90.5	92	94
1522	1557	1629	1647	1702	1777
1641	1679	1756	1775	1835	1915
1760	1800	1883	1904	1968	2054
1855	1897	1985	2007	2074	2165
1950	1995	2087	2110	2180	2276
1997	2044	2138	2161	2234	2332
2045	2092	2188	2213	2287	2387
2093	2141	2239	2264	2340	2443

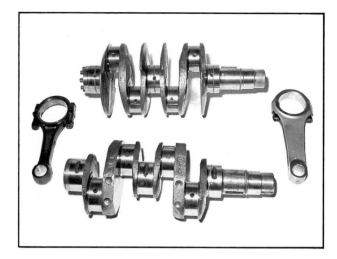

Stock crank at bottom, counterweighted stroker crank at top. The rod on the right side of photograph is a special 'Race Rod' from Dee Engineering.

If you are fitting a stroker crank, not only will you need to clearance the case, but you will have to fit modified rods – note machining of cap.

the camshaft then instant destruction will occur on firing up your new engine.

Whatever clearancing you do, ensure that there are no sharp edges left: always radius off any corners, otherwise you run the risk of a localized stress fracture occurring and effectively scrapping the crankcase.

The use of a stroker crankshaft opens up a whole new world of potential but easily surmountable problems. First of all, it doesn't take too much to realize that if the piston travels further up and down the bore and if nothing is done to lengthen the cylinder the piston will pop out of the top of the bore and slam into the head. You either have to fit spacers under the barrels or use special longer 'stroker' barrels, shortened pistons or a combination of both. What you need to end up with is a deck height – i.e. the distance between the top of the piston and the end of the barrel at top dead center – of 0.060in, or at least something very close. Reducing this figure can almost ensure valve to piston clearance problems and run the risk of the piston contacting the head at high revs, whereas a figure greater than this can reduce the 'squish' that is so desirable for efficient combustion.

Stroker cranks will also mean that you'll need to use different length pushrods. But then, as you will almost certainly have been machining the cylinder head anyway to get the desired compression ratio, you'll already be in the realms of cutting pushrods to length. When you set pushrod length, do so with a dummy adjustable rod which can be used to determine exactly the length required. By careful adjustment you should be able to come up with a rod that makes the rocker arm contact the valve stem dead center at half valve lift. You may still need to use some shims under the rocker shafts to gain the correct geometry, but don't be tempted simply to take a set of pushrods and rocker gear out of their respective boxes and slip them on hoping everything will be perfect first time. It won't be.

Always replace the stock aluminum pushrods when tuning the engine, especially if you are using a high-lift camshaft and heavy-duty valve springs. The stock items always flex under load. Most VW shops sell aftermarket chrome-moly pushrods, but check to make sure that they really are chrome-moly and not mild steel. Not everyone is as scrupulous as you might hope.

Using a stroker crank also means that you will need to stretch the stock pushrod tubes to fit and possibly modify the cooling tinwork as the cylinder heads will now be wider apart (unless using a 'modest' stroker crank and special shorter 'stroker' pistons). If you are still using a single center-mounted carburetor it may be that the intake manifold will be too short. Many aftermarket carburetor kits come with longer than stock center sections that can be cut to length, but check first.

To get the most from your 'stroker' motor you will have to go for a dual carb system. With an engine of over 1800cc virtually anything is possible, dual 44IDF Webers being particularly suitable for two-liter motors. Even 48IDA Webers can work on the street if you really do want to confound the opposition, but like we said earlier, don't expect good mileage from them.

Now's the time to take a look at the transmission. The stock VW trans is surprisingly strong and capable of handling much more power than was ever intended. However, as soon as you start playing drag racers at the lights, or begin to put 150 horsepower or more through the transmission, then something is going to give, usually the differential.

You will need to replace the stock diff with a so-called 'Super-Diff' which has an extra set of spider gears and a heavier differential housing. You should also replace the stock side plate on the transmission case with an aftermarket heavy-duty part. This will help keep the crownwheel and pinion together under extreme conditions.

If you shift gears hard, the stock shifter fork can bend, so replace it with a special heavy-duty one.

There are many specialist parts available for VW transmissions and it would be possible to write a book on that subject alone. Similarly, VW engine tuning is a massive topic, far outside the scope of one chapter in this book. What we have endeavored to do is give an indication of what it takes to build a hot street engine. The rest is up to you (and your wallet!).

If you have stayed with this up to now then you will have a pretty hot motor in your Bug – more than enough to blow the doors of most so-called sportscars at the stop light. This is what hotting up a VW motor is all about: surprising people when they discover that the innocent-looking Bug in the next lane isn't quite what it seems.

Experience the pleasure of seeing off a Porsche once and you're hooked for life.

Autocraft hi-ratio rocker assemblies are a popular choice for racers as they feature roller-bearings. Note wide rocker arm pad to prevent wear.

Setting up rocker gear requires use of a dial gauge. Check the position of rocker arm pad on valve stem and add shims to correct as necessary.

Any worthwhile increase in power output will put a strain on the clutch. Unit on left is heavy-duty spring type, while other is stock diaphragm.

The ultimate induction system? Kawell Racing Engines of Santa Ana supplied this race turbocharger set-up for the author's drag race Beetle.

VW engines can look very pretty – and very mean. This dual-Webered motor is ready to be slipped into a street Bug. Do not copy oil-cooler location.

TURN AND STOP
Making your Bug handle and halt

Apart from its flat-four air-cooled engine, the other principal technical feature that sets the VW Beetle apart from so many other cars is the suspension system. Unimpressed with the harsh ride given by conventional leaf springs, especially when used on small, lightweight cars, Dr Porsche turned to the torsion bar as a logical solution. A torsion bar is a spring consisting of a straight bar of tempered metal which is fixed at one end and resists any twisting force exerted on the other. The more it is twisted, the more it tries to resist. Torsion bars therefore not only have the added benefit of allowing a compact suspension design but they also act as rising-rate springs, i.e. the more the suspension is deflected the greater the spring rate becomes.

Apart from the late Super Beetles (1302 and 1303 models) which have MacPherson strut front suspension, all Beetles have torsion bar front and rear ends. The front suspension of a torsion-bar Bug consists of two parallel tubes running across the car, each housing a composite torsion bar made up of a number of thin strips, or leaves. These leaves are secured in the centre of each tube by a large socket-head bolt and locknut. From each end of the torsion bars are hung the trailing arms on to which the stub axle assemblies mount.

On pre-'66 Bugs, the up and down movement of the suspension is handled by the use of link-pins – in effect horizontally mounted kingpin assemblies – while later models (aside from the MacPherson strut cars) rely on conventional balljoints. Early cars use kingpins to act as steering pivots.

As far as the torsion bars themselves are concerned, the only real differences between early and late cars lie in the number of torsion leaves used, and the width apart of the two torsion bar tubes. Pre-'66 cars feature six individual torsion leaves in each tube, while later models have four large leaves and six small ones. For this reason it is not possible to change trailing arms from a later balljoint car to an older link-pin model. Don't forget, too, that you cannot change over the entire front axle assembly because the torsion bar tubes are a different width apart on the two models. So if you were planning on fitting a late disc-brake suspension assembly to your oval-window Bug, sorry, you're out of luck, unless you wish to change the entire floorpan, or cut the frame head off your chassis and weld on a new one.

There are generally reckoned to be five different ways to lower the front suspension of a torsion-bar Bug, ranging from the crude to the infinitely adjustable. Starting with the crudest first, you can get away with lowering by, in effect, reducing the overall springing at the front. This is done by removal of some of the torsion leaves from one or both torsion tubes.

In the case of link-pin models, you must remove all the torsion leaves, clean them thoroughly and then run a bead of arc weld across the leaves either side of the central retaining bolt, and a few inches in from each end, thus tying the leaves together. Next you have to cut out some of the leaves – usually two or three from each tube – leaving their remains still welded in place in the center and at each end. The idea of this is so the remaining pieces act as the necessary packing for the locating bolts to work properly. Reassemble and you have a lowered front beam.

To carry out the equivalent operation on a balljoint front end, you don't need to use a welder as the leaves are of different sizes. Just pull out the small leaves, cut off a few inches from each and tap them back into the trailing arms to act as packing for the locating bolts.

In this day and age, such a method of lowering cannot really be recommended, especially as there are now far better ways of carrying out the lowering process, ones which allow for complete adjustability.

A slight improvement over the above is the tried and true cut-and-turn method. You will need to remove the entire front axle beam from the car and then disassemble. Using a hacksaw, or better still a pipe-cutter, cut through the upper and lower torsion tubes about two inches either side of the central locating bolt. Clean up the edges of the cut – grind back any paint to bare metal – and then reweld the piece you've just cut out after rotating it so that the locating bolt ends up about half an inch below the original position. This has the effect of simply rotating the whole torsion bar and trailing arm assembly in relation to the rest of the front suspension system. If you are building a Baja Bug or another form of off-road VW, then you can use this same process to raise the car by rewelding the central mounting so that the locating bolt is about half an inch above the original position.

The great advantage of this form of lowering over the previous method of removing torsion bar leaves is that the strength of the front end is not affected at all. There have been cases of Beetles running around with no more than one solitary torsion leaf handling the suspension chores in each tube. Needless to say, that is nothing short of dangerous for it is the torsion bars that actually locate

To get a Beetle this low at the front will need more than a sack of potatoes in the trunk! Lowering a VW improves both looks and handling.

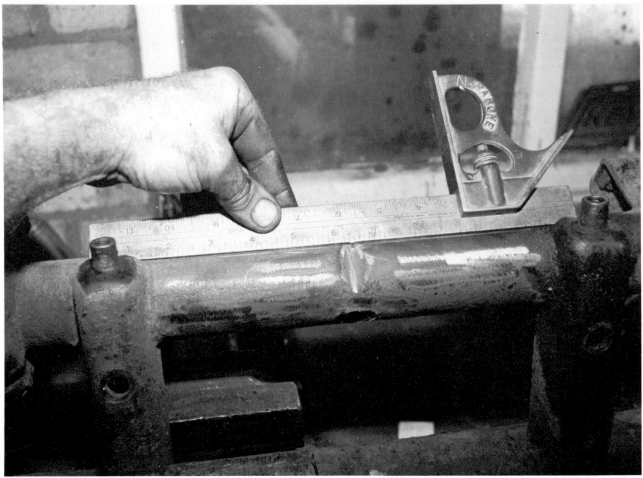

the trailing arms. If that one leaf should fail – and they can do with age – then suddenly you have major problems. Think safe.

The first method of lowering to come along that actually worked quite well was the Select-A-Drop which, as the name implies, offers a degree of adjustability. It is a crude device but one that offers a great improvement over the two previous methods.

It consists of a pair of U-brackets through which pass a pair of heavy bolts. Each bolt is drilled to allow another smaller bolt to pass through. To fit the Select-A-Drop, you again have to remove the entire front axle beam and completely disassemble it. Cut through the top tube two or three inches either side of the central locating bolt, having first of all welded in place one of the two large U-brackets. The second U-bracket is welded to the lower axle tube. Do not cut the lower tube. Now weld a pair of semi-circular guide plates (supplied with the complete kit) to the piece of tube you cut out of the beam across the saw cuts, but do not weld to the main axle assembly. These act as guide pieces when lowering.

The next step is to reassemble the torsion leaves in the axle beam and then pass the remaining smaller bolt through the two larger ones which are already in the U-brackets. Once the axle beam is remounted on the car, and everything else bolted back on, you will find that by tightening the small bolt which passes through the two

top left
Any lowering other than removal of torsion bar leaves will mean having to take the front suspension off the car. Access is gained under fuel tank.

left
When carrying out any kind of modification to the axle beam it is very important to measure everything carefully before you make that first cut.

above
Note how the torsion bar assembly has been cut either side of the central locating bolt, turned a few degrees and then rewelded to lower the Beetle.

below
The old Select-A-Drop lowering system was crude, but it worked. This was the first device that allowed the ride height to be adjusted to taste.

A torsion bar adjuster ready to be welded into a front beam. The nut on top clamps the whole lot tight, while the bolt on the side is used to lower the Bug.

larger ones, the front of the car will come down. What is happening in effect is that the upper torsion bar mounting is being forcibly dragged down towards the lower (fixed) one. Doing this pulls the torsion bar leaves round and they in turn twist the trailing arms upwards, thus lowering the car. It sounds a little complicated to explain, but in practice is a very simple device. It does have the drawback, however, of making the ride very choppy as one set of torsion bar leaves is fighting against the other the whole time, making the suspension very stiff.

The one adjustable lowering device that does not require any welding at all is the bolt-on Select-A-Drop which, as the name suggest, is designed to be fitted without recourse to anything more than spanners. For the lover of the radically low-riding Cal Look Bug, the biggest drawback with this device is that it won't drop the car by more than a couple of inches. However, for the owner who wants simply to improve the handling of his VW without going all the way into the weeds, this could be the answer. One big advantage is that, as it actually ties the two opposite lower trailing arms together, it acts as an anti-roll bar at the same time.

The fifth and final method (well, for the time being, until someone comes up with yet another system!) just happens to be the most popular on the market – the torsion bar adjuster or Sway-A-Way as it is frequently referred to. In fact, Sway-A-Way is the brand name of an American company which manufactures suspension products of many types, but the name has become almost synonymous with lowering kits.

Once again, you must remove the entire front axle assembly from the car and strip it down, removing torsion leaves and trailing arms. Measure the width of each adjuster and cut the torsion bar tubes equidistant either side of the central locating bolts, with the width between the cuts being the same as the width of the adjusters. Remove and discard the original locating bolts facing towards the front of the beam. Tack weld into place and when you are satisfied that the adjusters are correctly aligned, weld finally.

Reassemble the torsion leaves in the tubes as per the instructions supplied, and then remount the beam on the car. Add the trailing arms, stub axles, brakes, steering and wheels and you're away. To adjust the ride height, undo the locking nuts on the adjusters and wind the suspension up or down with an Allen key. The degree to which you can lower the car will be dependent on the angle at which you weld the adjusters into the beam. The further down they are, the lower you will be able to go. Obviously Baja and Buggy owners will want to weld them a little further up the other way to allow for an increase in ride height.

Lowering with torsion bar adjusters is simplicity itself – just unlock the clamp nut and then use an allen wrench to turn the adjusting bolt.

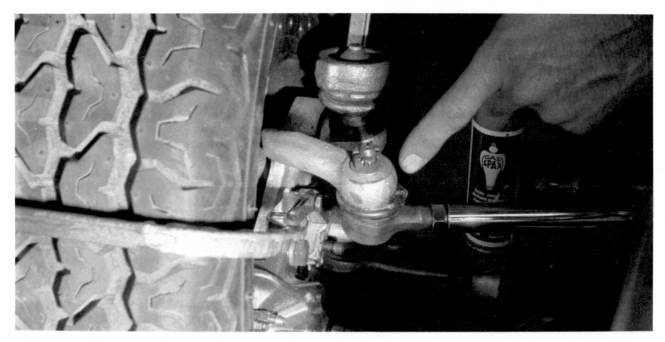

The great thing about this type of component is the range of adjustment available and the fact that the strength of the front end is not significantly affected.

Right, before we go any further, let's look at some important things to bear in mind when lowering a Bug. Did you know that there is a minimum legal height for headlamps? Believe it or not, the Bug's lights are just about as low as many countries allow, even before you set about creating a ground-hugging Cal Looker. If you have to put your VW through an annual inspection, it could be that it might fail because of the lights being too low. Check it out first, but don't forget that with torsion bar adjusters or a Select-A-Drop you can always wind the ride height up as necessary, and then back down again afterwards, but don't tell anyone we said so!

Do not forget that when you drop the suspension you will have to fit shorter shock absorbers, otherwise you will run the risk of the dampers continually bottoming out. On balljoint cars this is no problem at all as the shocks include the bump stops, so changing the units for special short ones will also help restore suspension travel. Link-pin front-end cars have separate bump stops mounted directly on to the torsion beam assembly. You may have to heat the metal part of the stop and bend it up out of the way slightly to gain some more wheel travel – not too much or you will end up relying on the fully compressed shock absorber to act as a limiting device. That would be one way of destroying your new shocks in double-quick time.

Another thing to consider on a '65-on car is the angle of the balljoints. Unlike link-pins which have an almost limitless angle of movement, balljoints have a very restricted angle through which they can move before they can move no more. Standard balljoints are obviously only designed to operate through the angles required by suspension riding at the factory-designed height. By dropping the suspension radically, you are in effect making the balljoints act as though the stock suspension is at full compression. Try to go much further and the balljoints could bind and at worst actually fail, with dire consequences.

Tie-rods can foul the underside of the fuel tank, causing a rattling while driving along, and even wear

Excessive lowering can induce bump steer so use a 'bump steer kit' to correct the problem, which allows the tie rod end to be fitted from below the arm.

through to cause a fuel leak. Extra clearance can be gained by fitting some spacers around the edge of the fuel tank, but a better solution is achieved by the following modification which also prevents, or at least reduces, bump steer.

Bump steer is caused by the tie-rods being forced to take on an unnatural angle either by the suspension being compressed when driving over a bump, or through the suspension being lowered. What happens is that as the wheels rise, they lift the tie-rods up at their outer ends, altering the angle at which they operate. As they rise, the ends describe an arc and effectively

If your front end is lowered more than a couple of inches it will be necessary to fit shorter shock absorbers like the one on the left.

become closer to the centerline of the car. This causes the Pitman arms (steering arms from the stub axles) to be pulled in towards the center of the car with the result that the wheels adopt a splay-footed stance for an instant. The lower the car is to start with, the worse this becomes.

To bypass this problem, remove the tie-rod ends from the Pitman arms with a balljoint separater and ream out the tapered hole to accept an adaptor that allows the tie-rod end to be fitted from below the arm. This restores the standard angle of the tie-rod and cures the bump steer. It also moves the tie-rod away from the fuel tank, so you can kill two birds with one stone.

Bump-steer isn't the only aspect of the handling that can be changed by lowering: caster angles are altered when you lower a Bug, meaning that the self-centering effect can be affected, giving the car a slightly twitchy feel. To re-establish the correct angle, fit a pair of caster shims between the lower torsion bar tube and the frame head when you bolt the assembly back on to the car.

You would be well advised to check the routing of the flexible brake pipes when radically lowering your Bug. Like the standard balljoints, the brake pipes were only ever designed to be used on a car with standard suspension. Lowering will result in the pipes appearing slightly too long. Try to route them so that you don't end up with a large loop of pipe running close to the ground.

Another problem can be the standard anti-roll bar as fitted to Beetles from 1959 onwards. This clearly gets in the way of a Select-A-Drop lowering device, and can get in the way of the road on a very low Bug! Although it does seem to go rather against the whole concept of good handling, about the only thing you can do is leave it off. If the reduction in ride height isn't too great, a car fitted with a Select-A-Drop can have the anti-roll bar mounted upside down to clear things.

Finally, whenever you carry out any such modifications on your Bug, do take it along to a specialist to get the front end alignment set correctly. Nothing wears out your new Michelins faster than incorrectly aligned steering.

Turning our attentions to the rear of the car, there are only two ways you can lower or raise the back end, so life is a whole lot simpler! All types of Beetle have essentially the same type of suspension, the only difference being whether the car is of the swing-axle or IRS type. Swing axle suspension is that found on the majority of Bugs other than Super Beetles, with the exception of US-specification cars from the seventies and semi-automatic 'Stick-Shift' models. These, like the later 1302 and 1303 ranges, were fitted with the IRS or four-joint rear end. The latter term comes from the fact that each car has four constant-velocity joints in the rear end, two on each driveshaft to allow for suspension movement. Swing-axle cars have solid one-piece axles which pivot at the inner, gearbox, end.

The advantages of each are plain to see. The older swing axle suspension is cheaper to manufacture and is virtually maintenance-free save for replacement of the axle-gaiters, which always seem to leak on older cars. On the other hand, IRS four-joint rear ends offer far superior handling (swing-axles bestow vast amounts of camber change as the suspension is raised or compressed) but can require replacement of the CV joints from time to time. They allow easier removal of the transmission, as the driveshafts, wheels and brakes can all be left in place on the car.

Essentially, the rear suspension of a Beetle consists of transverse torsion bars with trailing arms, just as at the front end. The big difference is that, whereas the axle beam at the front has two sets of multi-leaf torsion bars mounted in tubes, one above the other, and therefore a pair of trailing arms each side, the rear has two solid torsion bars, one for each side of the car. Each bar is fixed at one end (the inner end) by a set of splines, while the outer end is allowed to rotate in a rubber bushing. This end too is splined to accept the single trailing arm that carries the rear hub and brake assembly.

In reality the trailing arm at the rear is more than just a means of tying the hub to the torsion bar: it also acts as a spring, and for that reason its true name is the spring plate, it being a flat plate as opposed to a casting like those at the front. As the rear suspension is deflected, the spring plate twists the torsion bar but in doing so is twisted itself, adding to the springing effort. It is a very simple yet very sophisticated design.

Because the swing-axle type of suspension has a rigid tube over the axle that limits sideways movement of the hub assembly, the spring plate is the only other means of locating the outer end of the assembly. On an IRS system, the CV joints are designed to allow for sideways movement to take into account the arc described by the outer end of the driveshaft when the suspension is deflected. Needless to say, this means that there is no positive means of laterally locating the rear hub – not good for handling! To cure this problem, VW added a third suspension component on IRS cars, the semi-trailing or A-arm. This is a fabricated component, rigidly fixed to the hub assembly, that pivots about a mounting welded to the torsion bar tube just outboard of the front transmission mount.

It does not take too much to realize that the IRS design is, in pure handling terms, a far superior system. Whereas the swing-axle rear end brings about severe camber changes (note how a radically lowered early Bug always has a lot of negative camber at the rear end), the later IRS system is designed in such a way as to virtually eliminate any such change, though the A-arm will induce a small amount of camber change.

To lower the rear of a Bug is a relatively simple matter of removing the trailing arms from the torsion bar and moving them round by one or two splines. Well, that's the theory anyway. In practice it's a little more difficult, as you might imagine. Let's take a look at swing-axle Bugs first.

Start by removing the rear wheels, having securely located the car on axle stands on firm level ground. With a chisel, mark the relative positions of the rear hub assembly and spring plate so that when you reassemble the suspension you do not lose the factory-set toe-in setting. Undo the three 19mm bolts that hold the outer end of the axle to the spring plate and then also undo the shock absorber bottom mounting. On cars fitted with the Z-bar stabilizer, lift the mounting for this out of the way. Now undo the four 14mm bolts that retain the cover plate over the outer end of the torsion bar. Remove the cover and the bushing inside. With the aid of a trolley jack, lift the spring plate off the rebound stop and gently lever it free, but not so far as to pull the torsion bar out of its housing. Let the jack down and allow the spring plate to settle at its free angle. Take great care doing this as the spring plate is under great pressure from the torsion bar. If in any doubt, wrap a chain round the assembly to limit

When lowering rear end, always mark original position of trailing arm on torsion bar with paint so that you have a reference point.

Take care when removing the trailing arm not to dislodge the inner set of splines. You may need to use a puller to get the arm off.

any possible movement of the spring plate.

Either with a chisel, or with the aid of some white paint, mark the relative positions of the spring plate and the torsion bar. Coax the spring plate off the torsion bar's splines by gently tapping the torsion bar, and remove the spring plate altogether. Now replace it on the splines one spline up from its previous position – or down if you wish to raise the car – and reassemble. You may have problems getting the torsion bar cover plate back on to the end of the torsion bar, but try using a pair of longer bolts to first draw the cover into position. You will also find that the spring plate will foul against the rebound stop, so with a trolley jack gently pre-load the spring plate and lift it on to the stop. You can also use coil spring compressors for this job.

Lowering the IRS rear end is carried out along much the same lines, with the exception that you have the A-arm to contend with. You must undo the inner end of this A-arm at the bushing mounted on the torsion bar tube. You may then proceed as for the swing-axle cars.

If you find that severe lowering of an IRS has caused static negative camber of the rear wheels, you can get back to square one, in camber terms, by carrying out the following modification. Cut off the shock absorber mounting from each A-arm and make sure you mark the mountings 'left' and 'right' according to which side of the car they came from. Now remove the A-arms and swop them over, side for side. Next, reweld the shock absorber mountings back in exactly the same position relative to the chassis – simple, eh? The reason for this is that although the two A-arms look superficially the same, their inner and outer ends are not aligned the same way. Swopping the two over brings back a degree (excuse the pun) of positive camber to the rear end.

To improve the standard suspension, it is possible to replace all the standard rubber bushings with high-performance urethane moldings which not only refuse to compress like rubber, but remain self-lubricating at all times. The feel of a car fitted with urethane bushings throughout is more 'sporting', with a sharpness of handling unattainable with a standard Bug. Add to this a set of high-performance dampers such as those marketed by companies like Koni or Spax, and suddenly the Bug takes on a whole new feel. The great thing about these shocks is that they are fully adjustable for damping rate. Set them stiff for sports car handling, softer for everyday use.

If it's complete adjustability of the suspension you are after, then replace the standard spring plates with adjustable ones from Sway-A-Way. With the aid of a wrench it is possible to finely tune the rear suspension by raising or lowering it at will. With a matching adjustable front end, a set of Koni dampers and a few hours to spare, you can turn the Bug into a fine handling car, despite what everyone else says.

Take things a stage further still and fit a heavy-duty anti-roll bar to the front end, and an aftermarket rear anti-roll bar too. By now you will have a Bug that can outhandle many so-called sporty cars. That is fun!

Swopping the A-arms over side for side will rid a low IRS rear end of negative camber but you will need to cut off and reweld the shock mounts.

Heavy duty torsion bar bushes are a great way to improve the rear end of a Bug. The stock rubber parts are too soft and easily deform with age.

below
The simplest way to raise or lower the rear suspension of your Bug is to fit a pair of adjustable trailing arms. They are adjusted with a wrench.

above
A rear anti-roll bar is a worthwhile fitment to any Bug with an IRS set-up. It is easily fitted and improves the handling to an amazing degree.

below
Rear disc brake conversion on this nicely detailed California Look Bug not only looks good but greatly improves stopping power of the vehicle.

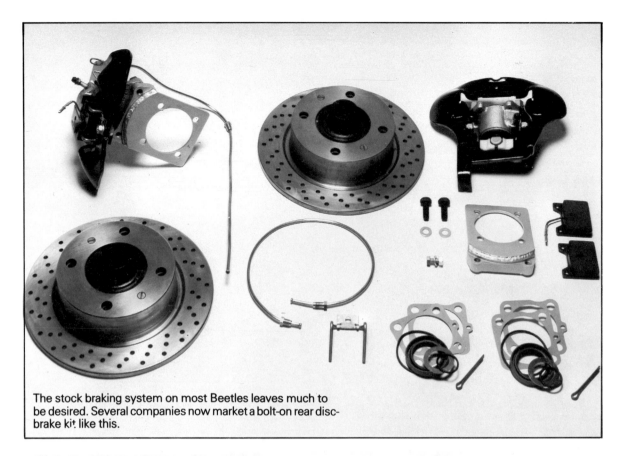

The stock braking system on most Beetles leaves much to be desired. Several companies now market a bolt-on rear disc-brake kit like this.

So you have now made the Bug go round corners to exploit the maximum from your new high-performance engine. Great, but what about the stopping power? Even the best handling car needs good brakes to get you out of trouble – and indeed to allow you to dive deeper into those corners in the first place. Now, although the Beetle's braking system can never be accused of being a state-of-the-art design, it can be made to perform very efficiently.

The early link-pin Bugs relied on drum brakes all round for stopping. The old Standard models even had cable-operated brakes – definitely room for improvement there! With the advent of the balljoint front suspension, VW started to think in terms of uprating the braking system. When they introduced the 1500 models in Europe in late 1966 (1967 model year), they finally made the move and incorporated disc brakes on the front of the Bug. For once the drivers of tuned VWs could expect their cars to stop on a dime – in theory, at least.

Owners of balljoint Bugs which don't have discs fitted as standard can uprate their braking by simply swopping over everything from the balljoints outwards with those components from a disc-braked car. Change the brake master cylinder too. You have to change the stub axles as those from a drum-braked car do not have the necessary mountings for the disc-brake calipers.

Sadly the owners of early link-pin models cannot fit factory disc brakes to their cars for there are no VW-manufactured parts available. However it is now possible, largely thanks to the demands of the off-road racing fraternity, to purchase bolt-on disc-brake conversions for link-pin front ends, but don't expect such luxuries to come cheap!

At the rear, disc-brake conversions are again available across the counter, but the main problem with some of these is that there is no provision for a cable-operated handbrake as is required by law in many countries. A popular conversion is fitting the rear disc-brake assembly from a Porsche 914 – not a simple bolt-on conversion, but one that requires a fair degree of engineering skill. However, those that have carried out such a conversion confirm that the end result justifies the necessary effort.

Although servo-assisted (power) brakes are possible on a Bug, the fact that the master cylinder is so far from the engine (the source of vacuum assistance) can cause more than a few problems. It is a feasible conversion, but bearing in mind that the Bug is not a heavy car it is doubtful that such a conversion is worth the effort.

One final way to improve the standard braking system is to replace all the flexible hosing with braided steel (Earl's, Aeroquip, etc.) hoses. This aircraft-quality hosing has a much higher burst pressure than the stock rubber type and resists 'ballooning' under pressure to a far greater degree. The result is a brake pedal that feels much firmer to the foot.

Finally, a word about wheels and tires. One of the worst things you can do to your Bug when searching for sports car handling is to over-tire it. When checking out the latest European supercars the Bug owner can get the impression that if wide tires are good for handling, fatter ones must be even better. Not so: the Bug already suffers from an understeering front end in the wet and over-tiring the car will make it even worse. The risk of aquaplaning in the wet is greatly increased, too.

The stock Bug came from the factory with 155-section radials. If 5½″ wide wheels (about the optimum for road use) are fitted, stay with nothing larger than 185/70x15

Rear disc conversion for a road car requires provision for a handbrake for legality. This conversion from UVA uses a stock Beetle brake cable.

tires. These have a section almost one inch fatter than stock but they do not over-tire the car in terms of width or overall diameter. The last point is especially important as the stock Bug gearing is designed so that 4th gear is almost like an overdrive. Increase the tire diameter too far and the workload becomes more than the stock engine can handle, as the overall gearing will be significantly increased. If for visual appeal (when building a low'n'fat custom, say) you do want to run extra fat tires, try to go for ones with a low aspect ratio (50-series for example) which will allow you to go wide in section without increasing the overall diameter too much. Remember, you will have to fit fatter fenders to compensate, as the stock parts will not accommodate really fat wheels and tires.

All the above modifications affect the safety of the car – for the better if carried out correctly by a competent mechanic. However, any work that you do to a Bug's suspension or braking system has to be performed to a high standard or else you run the risk of the failure of a vital component. Needless to say this is guaranteed to happen at exactly the wrong moment. Do not perform any work on your brakes or suspension if you have any doubts about your abilities – leave it to a qualified VW expert. As they say, better safe than sorry.

Now all that remains is to go and enjoy the new-found handling and stopping capabilities of your VW.

THE SPORTING LIFE

On the strip, in the desert and on the track

Unlikely though it may seem in view of the purpose for which the VW was originally designed, the Beetle has had a remarkably varied and successful competition career. From the word go, even Dr Porsche realized that there was hope for the Bug in racing. He and many others in postwar Germany built special-bodied Bugs for competition, and his first aluminum-shelled racer became the forerunner of a whole host of exotic sports and race cars. Even the early 356 Porsche models clearly betray their VW Bug derivation, while the mighty Turbo of today still retains a transverse torsion bar suspension system originally derived from the Bug.

However, while Dr Porsche's thinking led him away from the basic Beetle as a competition machine, many people since have proved that there is life in the old Bug yet. Today the familiar Beetle shape can still be seen on drag strips, rallycross circuits, off-road courses, even rally stages. Somehow it just refuses to lay down and die.

Drag racing is a sport where, in America and increasingly in Europe and Scandinavia, the Beetle has found a true home. The story goes back a long way to when people like Joe Vittone, founder of EMPI, took a look at the class rules and realized that there was a lot of potential in the VW. Already speed equipment was becoming available, thanks to the demands of customers who couldn't resist messing with their Bugs. In Germany, Okrasa produced a large range of specialist equipment to convert the humble 30-horse flat four into a somewhat healthier powerplant. With this and some domestically manufactured parts, the US enthusiast was able to build a useful engine with which to have fun.

However, serious drag racing is a bit more than just having fun, and it wasn't long before people like Vittone and Gene Berg began experimenting with some far more radical engine tuning parts. Suddenly the opposition had to sit up and take notice. Those funny Bugs didn't seem quite so amusing any more.

The beauty of the VW as far as drag racing is concerned centers around the traction advantages offered by a rear engine location. This places the maximum amount of weight over the rear driven wheels, so helping to reduce wheelspin off the line. The fact that the vehicle was light in weight didn't hurt either. Reading the class structures carefully it soon became obvious that with a healthy engine, the People's Car could take on the big guys on home territory, the drag strips of America, formerly the sole domain of the V8-engined muscle cars.

When the famous 'Inch Pincher' drag Bug first hit the strips, the effect was dynamite. Never before had anyone seen a car so small win so often, and with times that would put many a bigger-engined car to shame. The pattern was set for many years to come.

Today the drag Bug is very different from those of the early days. Back then the typical race car ran a full factory floorpan with a body that was stock other than 'glass fenders, deck lid and maybe doors. Interior-wise you would find a pair of race seats, a roll-over bar, tachometer, special shifter and an extinguisher. Many cars still retained much of the factory trim simply because the class weight breaks meant that excessive lightening was unnecessary.

Wheels were almost always the desirable EMPI-BRM mags, shod with slicks at the back and skinnies at the front, while for the engine it was a case of restroked VW crank, 88mm barrels and pistons, hot cam, reworked stock heads and dual 48IDA Webers from a V8.

With a beefed up transmission running close-ratio gearing, by the late sixties and very early seventies these Bugs were turning sub-12-second times at over 110mph. Not bad when you consider that a Porsche Turbo only covers the standing start quarter mile in the mid-13-second bracket today.

As the search for greater performance continued, it became obvious that the secret of quicker drag strip times lay not only in increased engine output but in more advanced chassis technology. The basic Bug becomes increasingly unstable as speeds rise over the 100mph mark – the back end tends to lift, causing the car to pivot about the front wheels. Chassis twist when leaving the line, thanks to 200 or more horsepower being put through a driveline originally designed for no more than one quarter of that amount, led many to think in terms of running a scratch-built chassis. Not only do you gain a weight advantage, but you have a more rigid structure to rely on.

It is this sort of thinking that has led to the current crop of Pro-Sedan machines which, despite an external shape that suggests 'Beetle', are pure race cars under the skin. The tube-chassis cars are capable of running quarter miles in well under 11 seconds at speeds approaching 130mph. It should be remembered that the engines are

State-of-the-art (at least at the time of writing!) are the tube-framed Pro-Sedans. Without turbochargers or nitrous oxide they run 10s.

modified flat fours running without turbochargers or the benefit of nitrous oxide injection. That is fast!

The other trend that is current at the time of writing is the full-floorpanned turbo race car. The advent of the turbocharger on the VW race scene has turned things upside down, for the flat four responds well to force-feeding by this means. Quarter miles covered in less than ten seconds are not uncommon with this type of machine.

The great thing about drag racing at grass roots level is that even the owner of a stock Bug can have fun bracket racing – this is handicap drag racing with qualifying times determining the degree of handicap. This way, a Bug capable of running only 20-second times can compete against a 12-second racer thanks to an 8-second head start. Fun for the participants and fun for the spectators as the faster car chases off down the strip trying to catch the slower Bug.

Rallycross and autocross are altogether different sports, being off-road short-circuit events popular in Europe. The Bug has traditionally held its head high in such racing thanks to the superior traction offered by the rear engine – that is until everyone discovered four wheel drive. Nowadays the top running Beetles are all using four wheel drive, with Porsche transmission modified to allow a power take-off to the front wheels. A much modified BMW differential unit at the front is a common solution to the problem of getting power to the wheels.

Essentially the cars are extensively lightened and modified Bugs, with much attention paid to safety and strength. Roll cages tied into the suspension mountings not only serve to increase driver safety but also help to make the lightweight vehicles far more rigid. Anything and everything that can be done to save overall weight is tried, from the usual 'glass fenders and other body panels to plastic windows, drilled brackets, lightweight aluminum components and split-rim wheels.

top right
Rallycrossing can be hard on a car, especially if it has 'glass fenders! The rear engine aids traction and makes for spectacular driving styles.

right
Geoff Thomas's old rallycrosser was ultra-light. Ears on side were for ram cooling of engine, a 2.1-liter 'stroker' with dual 48IDA Webers.

With the benefit of a rear-mounted engine, the Beetle has superb traction off the line. As you can see, things can get a little out of hand!

Engine-wise, many cars in the past have featured modified VW Type 4 engines, which can be bored and stroked out to 2.7 liters or more. Turbocharger systems are commonplace on such engines. However, in the past the Bug has been very successful on the rallycross circuits running modified Beetle engines of 2.1 or more liters with dual 48IDA Weber carbs and thoroughly conventional tuning throughout. Even with this relatively unsophisticated set-up the cars were extremely competitive against many far more powerful race cars.

Although the Bug may have had a glorious past in rallycross, it would be true to say that these days the more advanced four wheel drive machinery derived from Audi, Ford and BMW vehicles tend to lead the way. But don't expect the Bug to take it all lying down. There's plenty of fight left yet!

Rallying is another area in which the Bug has not really had much success in recent years, largely because many rallies have been reduced to outright speed tests against the clock, in sharp contrast to the trials of endurance they once were. At club level there are many cars available which lend themselves to inexpensive modification and they have proved more popular than the Beetle, for all its attributes. In the early Seventies the works teams from Porsche Austria, driving highly developed 1302S models, were front runners in the European championship series, and at club level in Europe, many people cut their rallying teeth driving Beetles, finding that their ruggedness more than made up for the lack of outright horsepower.

However, despite the lack of popularity these days, there is no reason why a budding club rally driver shouldn't have a lot of fun driving one of these idiosyncratic little cars. It would liven up the conversation in the paddock if nothing else!

There are two areas of off-road sport, however, where the Bug can still hold its head up high: production car trials and full-blown off-road desert racing.

The former is a trial held usually on muddy, hilly terrain' where the object of the proceedings is to complete a complex and difficult course without stopping or touching the course markers. The trial requires a lot of skill on the part of the driver, and a delicate right foot if wheelspin is to be avoided. Traction thanks to a rear engine is where the Beetle scores. While there have been many cars built over the years that would appear to lend themselves well to trialling, few have matched the success of the Bug. With its smooth floorpan it is difficult to get hung up on roots and rocks, while the large diameter wheels help the Beetle to paw its way over rough terrain.

The fact that the suspension system is so easily modified for an increase in ride height is another big plus point, for trials cars need all the ground clearance they can get. With a passenger on board to help with the traction by bouncing up and down on the rear seat (really!) and two spare wheels strapped to the back, the trials Bug may present a strange sight to someone used to Cal Look cruisers, but it is an effective device with a winning history.

left
The Beetle used to be a front-runner in the rallying world in Europe, but nowadays they are few and far between. Ruggedness helped a lot.

right
Production car trials are tests of off-road skill where you need to climb difficult slopes without coming to a halt or straying off course.

below
What other 'stock' car would you ever see on the startline of the Mint 400 off-road race? This Bug looks right at home at the head of the line.

In America, indoor short-course off-road racing is very popular, with many front-running cars being Volkswagen powered like this Chenowth.

Off-road desert racing is a natural habitat of the Beetle. For years VW-based racers dominated the desert racing scene in Southern California and Mexico, giving rise to the birth of the Baja Bug – so called because its roots lie in the Baja 1000 off-road race held each year in the Baja peninsular. The short-fendered, Bug-bodied racers lent themselves well to the rigors of serious off-road competition thanks to their rugged construction, rear engine location and overall tough constitution.

There are many companies specializing in selling off-road race parts for Beetles and because of this there is no other vehicle that can compete so effectively, especially bearing in mind cost factors. Certainly preparing a race-ready off-road Baja is not cheap, but it can be a lot less expensive than choosing to build a specialist tube-chassis car. However, if it is outright strength, light weight and good handling that you seek, then there is no substitute for the off-road 'rail'.

This type of machine has become highly developed in the USA, where it is almost the Grand Prix car of off-roading. Complex multi-tube chassis, multiple-shock suspension systems with incredible wheel travel, ultralight wheels, special race tires, bullet-proof transmissions and very highly developed race engine all go to make the purpose-built desert racer an extremely impressive device.

At a more down to earth level, short-course racing has been popular in America for some years and is gaining in popularity in Europe too. The vehicles used are almost all VW-derived and as such can be relatively inexpensive to build. That does not mean to say, however, that they are slow, or the racing boring for the spectator. Far from it. With vehicles literally flying over

Flying Baja Bug of Keith Felstead uses relatively stock 1600cc Beetle engine as rules do not allow anything else. The cars still fly though.

top right
Autotesting is a popular Sunday pastime for some enthusiasts, with many Beetles appearing over the years. Peter Noad's was the most successful.

right
Oops! Sometimes things go wrong, no matter what the sport. Formula Vee car was in collision with trackside barrier and sadly came off second best!

man-made jumps and fighting wheel to wheel with the opposition, the racing is close and extremely exciting.

Far from desert racing or drag strip action is the world of driving tests – no, not the examination you have to go through to get a driving licence, but a test of driving skill whereby a course is marked out with cones or pylons, the aim being to drive that course as quickly as possible without touching any markers. Failure to complete the course without dislodging a cone renders the competitor liable to an extra time penalty.

The driving test – or autotest as it is also known – is very popular in parts of Britain and over the years VW Beetles have proved very successful. The main requirements of an autotest car are that it should be very maneuverable, easily thrown around and brisk off the mark. At first sight it would be easy to think that the Beetle is anything but maneuverable, 'chuckable' and brisk, but experience has proven that this is not the case. With some basic engine and suspension mods and, it has to be said, a skilled driver, the Bug can be a winner.

An off-road rail flying round the course — literally it seems.
These machines are very light and yet extremely strong.

In the USA, the similar but more specialized slalom racing has proved a popular hunting ground for much-modified Bugs in the past, proving yet again that there is seemingly no end to the VW's versatility. Or is there? How about single-seater circuit racing? Surely not. Well, even on the tarmac tracks there have been Beetle-derived racers throughout the years, the ultimate being the Formula Vee cars. These are popular in Europe and frequently feature a purpose-built monocoque aluminium chassis on to which (the rules dictate) a VW torsion bar front suspension system is grafted, along with a Beetle engine and transmission at the rear.

The governing rules are strict, allowing a maximum engine capacity of just 1500cc, with a single carburetter venturi of restricted size per cylinder head (single-port heads only allowed), standard gear ratios and swing-axle transmission. Strict the rules may be, but they do help reduce the cost of the series as far as the competitor is concerned and they make for very close racing. The rules also ensure that the maximum amount of ingenuity is used when building a Formula Vee engine.

The Formula Vee series has been a popular one for many years in Britain and on an international level has acted as the springboard to success for many top names in motor sport. Once again, the humble Beetle proves its versatility.

Finally, who can resist mentioning the crazy 'Boss Beetle' circuit racer shown here. It may have a widened Formula 5000 chassis under the skin, and it may have a race-prepared Chevy V8 engine mounted amidships, but it is still unmistakably a Beetle. Now that is different!

left
Formula Vee racing relies on 1300cc engines with single-port heads and swing-axle suspension at rear. Mark Thomas races his Cavan 87 at Brands Hatch.

Boss Beetle – the name says it all. A Formula 5000 car under the skin, the 'Boss' is still instantly recognizable as a modified VW Beetle.

Adam Wik's 'Wikked' Pro-Sedan Bug warms its tires in readiness for a trip down the drag strip. These Pro-Sedans are extremely rapid machines.

USEFUL ADDRESSES

AUTOCAVAN (Custom & Performance components)
103 Lower Weybourne Lane
Badshot Lea
Farnham
Surrey
England
Tel: (0252) 333891

AUTOCRAFT (Specialist components)
1050 Cypress #K
La Habra
California 90631
USA
Tel: (714) 870-9797

GENE BERG (Performance components)
1725 North Lime
Orange
California 92665
USA
Tel: (714) 998-7500

BUGPACK (Performance Components)
Dee Engineering Inc
3560 Cadillac Avenue
Costa Mesa
California 92626
USA
Tel: (714) 979-4990

COMPOMOTIVE (Specialist wheels)
4-6 Wulfrun Trading Estate
Stafford Road
Wolverhampton
England
Tel: (0902) 311499

ENGLE (Camshafts)
1621 12th Street
Santa Monica
California 90404
USA
Tel: (213) 450-0806

GERMAN CAR CO (Custom & Resto components)
4-6 High Street
Hadleigh
Essex SS7 2PB
England
Tel: (0702) 551766

HOUSE OF HASELOCK (Restorations)
22 Slingsby Close
Attleborough Fields Estate
Nuneaton
Warwickshire
England
Tel: (0203) 328343

JSC (Custom & Performance components)
6411 Beach Blvd
Buena Park
California 90621
USA
Tel: (714) 522-6116

KAWELL RACING ENGINES (Turbochargers)
1320 E. St Andrew
Santa Ana
California 92705
USA
Tel: (714) 549-7276

LIMITED EDITION
(Custom & Performance components)
19 Melford Court
Hardwick Green
Warrington
Cheshire
England
Tel: (0925) 822226

Mr BUG (EMPI parts)
1202 W. Struck Avenue
Orange
California 92667
USA
Tel: (714) 633-1093

NEAL (Buggy controls)
7170 Ronson Road
San Diego
California 92111
USA
Tel: (714) 565-9336

PAUTER MACHINE (Specialist components)
367 Zenith St
Chula Vista
California 92011
USA
Tel: (714) 422-5384

PHOENIX (Exhaust systems)
3963 Alamo Street
Riverside
California 92501
USA
Tel: (714) 788-2361

RIMCO (Machining)
520 East Dyer
Santa Ana
California 92707
USA
Tel: (714) 549-0357

S&S (Exhaust systems)
1401 E. Ball Road
Anaheim
California 92805
USA
Tel: (714) 758-0355

SCAT (Custom & Performance components)
PO Box 1220
Redondo Beach
California 90278
USA
Tel: (714) 370-5501

SCS (Custom & Performance components)
618 E. Ball Road
Anaheim
California 92805
USA
Tel: (714) 635-6620

THUNDERBIRD (Exhaust systems)
Ermio Immerso Ent. Inc.
18700 Susana Road
Rancho Dominguez
California 90221
Tel (213) 537-1800

UVA (Custom & Performance components)
Argents Mere Hi-Tech Park
Hambridge Lane
Newbury
Berkshire
England
Tel: (0635) 33888

WEST COAST METRIC (Resto parts)
2323 W. 190th Street
Redondo Beach
California 90278
USA
Tel: (213) 376-9852

Racing Associations

750 Motor Club (Formula Vee racing)
Dave Bradley
16 Woodstock Road
Witney
Oxfordshire
England
Tel: (0993) 702285

VWDRC (Volkswagen drag racing)
VolksWorld Magazine
Link House
Dingwall Avenue
Croydon
CR9 2TA
England
Tel: (01) 686-2599

VW Magazines

DUNE BUGGIES & HOT VWs
Wright Publishing Co Inc
PO Box 2260
Costa Mesa
California 92628
USA

SUPER VW MAGAZINE
7 Rue de Lille
75007 Paris
France

VW TRENDS
McMullen Publishing Inc
2145 West La Palma Avenue
Anaheim
California 92801
USA

VOLKSWORLD
Link House Magazines Ltd
Link House
Dingwall Avenue
Croydon
CR9 2TA
England